# TO AN INSANE DEGREE

*A MEMOIR*

# TO AN INSANE DEGREE

*A MEMOIR*

SANDY DIAMOND

To An Insane Degree: A Memoir

Copyright © 2020 Gabriel Diamond and Sandy Diamond

All rights reserved. No part of this book may be reproduced in any form or by any means, electronic or mechanical, including photocopying, recording, or by any information storage and retrieval system, without permission in writing from the publisher.

Photography: Linda Koolish
Cover painting and calligraphy: Sandy Diamond
Cover design: Rob Allen @n23art

Library of Congress Control Number: 2020923849

First Edition

Oakland, California

The paper used in this publication meets the requirements of the American National Standard for Permanence of Paper for Publications and Documents in Libraries and Archives Z39.48-1992.

*"Form is a straitjacket in the way that a straitjacket was a straitjacket for Houdini."*

—Paul Muldoon, *The Irish Times*

# ACKNOWLEDGMENTS
*By Gabriel Diamond*

Rikki Ducornet spent countless hours with Sandy, editing and refining this memoir. Rikki was a generous friend and collaborator. This memoir might not have ever been finished if it weren't for her. Thank you, Rikki.

Christine Hemp, Erin Fristad, and the rest of Sandy's writing group gave her years of support and creative community and inspiration.

Denise Winter, director of Key City Players in Port Townsend for her support with play writing and giving Sandy's words a stage.

Candice Holdorf for the diligent and thoughtful copy editing and formatting and mostly the gentle, loving reminders to keep working on this.

Dianne Diamond, her ever-loving sister read through the text multiple times and used her incredible skills for details to find so many edits, resisting her urge to write in the margins "That's not how it happened!" when her own memories were different than my mom's. Sandy always stood for her right to take poetic license.

Diedre Hammons and Emily Crawford-Margison also provided copy editing and design assistance. The cover photo of Sandy Diamond was taken by Linda Koolish.

## CONTENTS

Acknowledgments *By Gabriel Diamond* ____ 7
Foreword *by Rikki Ducornet* ____ 15
In Memoriam *by Christine Hemp* ____ 17
Michael ____ 23
How to Starve ____ 24
Van Gogh in Cleveland ____ 25
Sooty with Love ____ 26
Bargain with God ____ 28
You Don't Have to Be Jewish ____ 30
What Was Going On in the World ____ 31
New York Steak ____ 32
How to Draw a Cow ____ 33
Famous Winter Night ____ 34
Gigi & Monet ____ 36
Sally ____ 37
Impasto & Glaze ____ 39
Not Like Other People ____ 40
Rilke in the Village ____ 42
Alterations ____ 43
The Size of a Pickle ____ 45
A Pot Big Enough to Put a Naughty Child into ____ 47
The Bracelet ____ 48
Don't Jump ____ 50
The Darkest Time ____ 51
Kerouac in the Asylum ____ 53
Dr. Caligari ____ 55
How the World Looked ____ 56
The Questioner ____ 58

| | |
|---|---|
| Once I Was a Rabbit | 59 |
| Buick, Cadillac | 60 |
| Second Grade | 61 |
| Breakdown | 62 |
| Visiting Hour | 63 |
| Montemartre | 64 |
| Dr. Jekyll & Mr. Hyde | 65 |
| Rilke in Ohio | 66 |
| The Cops: Gates Mills, 1960 | 69 |
| Coffin & Blood | 70 |
| Peggy & Buzzy | 71 |
| How to Draw a Nurse | 72 |
| Don't Crowd a Manic | 73 |
| Aunt Rose | 75 |
| Six White Horses | 76 |
| God's Countenance | 78 |
| My Song for Crazy Writers | 80 |
| The Comprehensive | 81 |
| Gimbel's | 82 |
| Charles the Gun Collector | 85 |
| Ingleside 1960 | 88 |
| The Road to Nantes | 93 |
| Braids Unraveled | 95 |
| No-Touch Hill | 98 |
| Still Life for Stan | 100 |
| Waterfall | 101 |
| Route 66 | 102 |
| 1956. Ain't We All? | 104 |
| The Alcazar | 106 |
| A Screamy Time of Year | 109 |
| Mona Lisa | 111 |
| Paint by Number | 112 |
| Where Were You? | 114 |
| Beverix | 115 |
| Memorial Day | 116 |
| All the Knives in Emergency | 118 |

| | |
|---|---|
| The Persian Rug | 120 |
| The Cast | 121 |
| Errol Flynn's Teeth | 123 |
| Marilyn Monroe | 125 |
| A Blue Sailing Ship | 126 |
| Beverixing | 128 |
| Nina Simone | 129 |
| The Turtle | 130 |
| Hunchback | 132 |
| An Inextinguishable Longing | 133 |
| The Hunchback of Notre Dame | 135 |
| The Journey Inside Them | 136 |
| The Jew-Hater's Trolley, 1946 | 138 |
| Beyond Repair | 140 |
| Little Sister, 1969 | 141 |
| The Egyptian Book of the Dead | 143 |
| Red Lace | 144 |
| Maxie | 145 |
| Madame Butterfly | 147 |
| Bootleg Massacre, 1930 | 148 |
| Eliot Ness and President Roosevelt | 149 |
| San Francisco Donuts, 1969 | 150 |
| Mistress of Peonies | 152 |
| Bring the War Home! | 154 |
| Levitating the Pentagon | 155 |
| The Salon of the Lord | 156 |
| Nighties | 157 |
| Shirley Temple Undressed | 158 |
| The Sniper | 159 |
| Tangerines Like Goldfish | 160 |
| Mistaken Identity | 161 |
| Nixon | 162 |
| I'll See You Again | 163 |
| Too Late for Addiction | 164 |
| The Orange Bowl Parade | 165 |
| I Am Here | 166 |

| | |
|---|---|
| Eternity | 167 |
| The Queen of England | 168 |
| Real Leather | 169 |
| Her Braids | 170 |
| The Ladies' Room, 1944 | 171 |
| Inheritance | 172 |
| The Greeting Card | 173 |
| Ann Sexton, "Rumpelstiltskin" | 174 |
| The Eyeless Earth | 175 |
| When Ohio Was Texas | 176 |
| Mary | 177 |
| Oakland, 1971 Medicine Man | 178 |
| The Heavens at the Time of Your Birth | 180 |
| Welcome to the Tasty Shop | 182 |
| Luck | 185 |
| The Guillotine | 186 |
| Wall Street | 188 |
| Earthquake | 189 |
| The Red Shoes | 190 |
| Bartleby | 192 |
| Ampersands of Love | 194 |
| What God Wants of Us | 195 |
| Quicksilver Pinions & Permanence | 196 |
| Monastery & Serifs | 197 |
| Chance | 199 |
| Einstein & Gertrude Stein | 200 |
| Graphology | 202 |
| How to Draw a Lion | 203 |
| Edgar Allan Poe | 205 |
| What is Green? | 206 |
| The Zodiac Streets | 207 |
| Guns-R-Us | 209 |
| Gullible | 210 |
| The Talking Heads | 211 |
| Tell It to the Marines | 212 |
| Letters Fell From His Sleeve | 213 |

| | |
|---|---|
| Haight Street | 215 |
| Mystifying Paths | 216 |
| Hitler's Socks | 217 |
| Gertrude & Alice & Sammy | 218 |
| Prove It's Right to Kill | 220 |
| Eucalyptus | 222 |
| The Last Beautiful Thing | 224 |
| Oregon | 228 |
| Women Who Had Done It All | 229 |
| Things Standing In For Other Things | 231 |
| Threads Once Sewn to Someone's Coat | 233 |
| The Yamhill River | 234 |
| Sleeping with Everyone In Sight | 235 |
| Primitive Life Forms | 236 |
| How to Be a Hunchback | 238 |
| Hunchback Movies | 240 |
| The Joke | 241 |
| Call It Your Life | 242 |
| When No One Was Looking | 243 |
| Sandy's Afterward | 244 |
| Epilogue *By Dianne Diamond* | *247* |
| Gabriel's Afterward *by Gabriel Diamond* | *249* |

# FOREWORD
*by Rikki Ducornet*

My friend and neighbor, Sandy Diamond, was a tiny, existentially muscled, funny, gifted, and luminous being. She was often outrageous, chronically flirtatious, sporadically irritable, and above all, irresistible. She was a poet, a painter, a playwright, a terrific performer. Her hump, so like the curse of a jealous fairy, she battled with grace and a ferocious sense of humor. Instants before the fall that broke her back, she had been sunbathing on a garage roof, a young beauty in a red and white polka dot bikini. When I met her, she was performing before a packed house with a band named Quasimodo and the Bellringers.

Visiting Sandy was like visiting a favorite aunty (tea and cake), a siren, a sister, and a stand-up comic all at the same time. Like her conversation, her memoir is sparked with stories : her father's deli—its menu and regulars, the terrible sadness of mental institutions, the confusions of family life, Peter Orlovsky in bed, road trips, motherhood, what it is like to be a painter on the verge of starvation reaching for a candy bar delivered to a second story window in a basket hanging from a rope. Unlike anything, Sandy's spirited memoir—which she worked on within hours of her death—is a small treasure of perturbation, tenderness, inspiration, uncommon pain and spirited resilience. I am happy I get to share it with you.

# IN MEMORIAM
*by Christine Hemp*

JULY 31, 1936–FEBRUARY 9, 2016

Poet, painter, playwright, performer, memoirist, calligrapher, friend, mother, sister, grandmother, diva, re-inventor of art forms, instigator of hilarity (as well as tears), Port Townsend jewel Sandy Diamond has died from complications resulting from a fall. She would have turned 80 in July. Her departure—on Mardi Gras, no less—crowned an enormous life housed in a diminutive frame.

Born in 1936 to Elizabeth and Samuel Diamond in Gates Mills, Ohio, Sandy was passionate about words and images from infancy. Her mother told her she was "scribbling on her crib sheet as soon as she was strong enough to hold anything that made a mark." She marked her way to Brandeis University where she studied literature, and then earned her BFA from Columbia University's College of Painting and Sculpture.

Her poem "The Story of My Life" begins Hike to think of myself as a born artist/What they call Art/was always there with me - not like a hobby or a career,/but like breath. New York offered Sandy the intoxication of living and breathing her art, but she also suffered severe manic-depressive episodes. A breakdown at 22 precipitated three trips to mental institutions. Thirty years later, these experiences would be fodder for her stirring, award-winning first book of poems, Miss Coffin and Mrs. Blood: Poems of Art & Madness: None of us would say their names./Not because of the ghastliness —An a situation like ours (put away put away put away)...But Coffin and Blood/the ancient twin attendants of our cure/neither dead nor alive, but artificial as cherries on a hat...

The Queen of Diamonds could always call a spade a spade.

If one infirmity were not enough, during that time Sandy was given another opportunity to turn misfortune into art. Born with curvature of the spine ("my mother always told me to sit up straight!"), the scoliosis was exacerbated by a fall from a roof. One afternoon, descending onto two stacked garbage cans after rooftop sunbathing (in a red-and-white laced bikini, she was quick to point out), one can tipped, and Sandy toppled. After months in a body cast, her broken back healed, but her spine continued to curve.

It was Sandy's great gift, however, to offer others a way to embrace what some might perceive as deformity. *I curve like a swan, like pianos/ like my mother's arm around me. I earned this back...* (from "Romeo and the Hunchback"). Sandy's robust ego and devotion to her art gave her the chutzpah to wow even casual observers. With wily charm, Sandy was known to make strapping men melt, bring women to their knees in laughter, and entertain children as well as her memorable cats. To behold Sandy was to experience an innately sensual person, a woman who claimed her body as well as her mind.

In 1969, when the physical demands of painting forced her to stop, Sandy moved west to Berkeley where she honed her talent in calligraphy—which she called "the bridge between literature and art." With her sister Dianne handling the business end, Sandy sold and exhibited her cards and fusions of written quotes, collages and painted images in the Bay Area, New York, and in private collections, including those of Gloria Steinem, Whoopi Goldberg, and the Dalai Lama. In 1986 she published a book of her calligraphic quotations from literature, *Bliss. Danger & Gods*.

Her fecundity did not stop with her art: At age 36 she wished for a child. *I'd been painting for fifteen years/full-time between bouts of madness. Painting was everything; I wanted more.* A man she only ever referred to as "The Medicine Man" gave her the child she longed for. *His father tried to give me money, a ring/but he'd already given me all I'd asked/I'm not saying I did it the best way. Medicine Man had backbone, plumage/and everything in between. /But I didn't feel sick.* (From "The Sign of Libra.")

Sandy reared her son in Berkeley and Oakland, encouraging his own artistic passions of dance, theater and filmmaking. When he left for college, Sandy moved to Oregon and turned to writing. In 1998, an artist residency at Port Townsend's Centrum, allowed her to compose her second collection of poems, The Hunchback. When people initially heard and read the poems, they thought they were performance pieces, that she should have a back-up band. When Centrum program manager Peter McCracken got wind of this, he hooked her up with local blues harmonica player David George Gordon, pianist and bassist Bruce Cannavaro and guitar player Bruce Cowen—just to see how the chemistry might work.

Within weeks "Quasimodo and the Bellringers" was performing at Siren's Pub, Portland's Artichoke Music and later at Seattle's Bumbershoot. Sandy moved to the City of Dreams and soon became the darling of Port Townsend, appearing with the Bellringers at the bustling Upstage Dinner Theater as well as benefits and weddings. When Upstage owner Mark Cole first heard Sandy and the Bellringers, he popped a bottle of champagne. Anyone who attended those gigs witnessed a well-greased and wildly talented combo: A tiny (ageless) woman with edgy irony delivering lines like a vaudeville pro; the bluesy, artful bass and guitar; a soulful harmonica offering grace notes to the surprising parsing of her poetic lines; sometimes a member of the band taking a line as well. All were riveting theater. The Hunchback poems were huge crowd pleasers, and Sandy basked in the applause. "The Hunchback in the Supermarket" begins "Just my luck, it's law of merchandising:/if it has a bird on it, it goes on the top shelf..." or from "Small People of America: A Press Conference": "Mostly we tell tall-people jokes...."

The Bellringers went on to cut two albums, What Madness Is and Still Life. A live performance was broadcast on NPR's "West Coast Live" and local station KPTZ still airs tracks.

But Sandy did not rest on her laurels. During her tenure in Port Townsend, she also wrote myriad one-act and full-length plays, winning seven awards at the local Playwrights Contest. Many were produced at the Key City Theater. After the Bellringers disbanded, when Sandy was well into her seventies, she went on to perform with a revolving crew of actors, musicians and writers, including a short-lived but sparkly cowboy-themed entourage called "Sandy Diamond and the Rhinestones."

Though fiercely competitive and a lover of the spotlight, Sandy was never one to brag. She held high the work of painters and poets who lit the way for her, and always supported and cheered her artist friends, making each one feel accomplished, successful, and special.

In her last days, when a friend complimented her on her fortitude, she threw a familiar sidelong glance, waved her delicate fingers, and with a glint in her eye quipped, "I'm trying to be noble." And noble she was till the end. On February 9, her son Gabriel sent an email to all those who loved Sandy. The subject line: "The Queen of Diamonds has folded her hand."

# TO AN INSANE DEGREE

# MICHAEL

*Michael and I played in the woods all day. Mother'd clang the cowbell, calling us home for dinner. We heard it past the swamp, where Grandfather grew horseradish for the Seder's bitter herb. If you stepped too close, you'd never be heard from again. Past the jack-in-the-pulpits, looking like a hundred little rabbis furled in their striped shawls, chanting "Magnified and sanctified be the name of the Lord"—magnified because the enemies of the Jews had shrunk them smaller than Christians. Sanctified because God had to stay up late to save America from the war. Past the seven-year trilliums that bloomed every year I was a child. If you picked one, its whorls would swallow your hand and suck you into the narrow stalk. Then you would be a white flower in a carpet of flowers, growing roots in the spongy earth. And when Mother and Daddy came looking for you, could your green throat say, "Look, look. It's me, Sandy, the second-born, the first girl. Find me?"*

# HOW TO STARVE

1958. Morningside Drive, Columbia University, on the way to my painting studio, off the catwalk radiating from Low Library's sacred dome. Smoking a long butt from the kindness of sidewalks. Reflected in the fruit stand window—was that me, staring at apples, picturing a still life to paint? Which apple is best? Which one is as rosy as a roadside apple when in Ohio I walked home from school with my brother a mile past the end of the bus line? Fruit hanging plump and shiny in the sun. Easy-pickin' back then. And free. My parents were against art school and New York in the first place—Mother saying to Dad, "I'm not paying for her to learn how to starve." Who is that reflected in the grocery window, cheeks sunken with Mother's prophecy? Was it just last year when people asked me, "Hey, are you pregnant?" This phantom in the glass, hand poised above the Red Delicious waiting for the right one to jump up to pose on a scrap of lace. Yes, lace—which pulsates and flings itself in violent openings. I have money for just one; an apple to paint, too red to steal.

I thought the creature in the glass was someone making fun of me, mimicking my every move, a stranger who would grab the apple I wanted to paint, bite into it, her teeth marks vicious in the white flesh, the fruit naked and weeping.

The stranger said, "No one's looking. Take it. You deserve it, darling. If you're arrested, I'll vouch for you. You're so thin. You look like those cardboard silhouettes cops use for target practice."

I'd eat that apple, but first I'd paint it. A still life—the mouth of a basket open to eat the fruit that is leaning against it. A cream pitcher, its handle skewed. Skim milk. Not the cream of home.

*Is this the same still life hanging in a dining room in the distant future when a visitor might ask, "What is this painting supposed to mean?"*

*Sandy Diamond*

# VAN GOGH IN CLEVELAND

The Cleveland Museum of Art and its swan-studded lagoon were a few blocks up Euclid Avenue from my parents' deli, the Tasty Shop. Saturdays, from my ninth year to my twelfth, my father, in his Chevy station wagon reeking of dill pickles, dropped me off at the museum's wide marble stairs. Up I'd go to the Class for Gifted Children. We learned how to paint with egg tempera as da Vinci did. That first year, the war was still on, eggs a luxury. Daddy built a chicken coop and stocked it with beautiful, squawking, clucking Rhode Island Reds. Eggs for the Tasty Shop, eggs for the family, eggs for The Gifted Children.

One day, the teacher gathered us around an oil painting in a gilded frame in the Post-Impressionist Room. Beneath an ultramarine sky, yellow street lamps and a scalloped awning gleamed a café scene by van Gogh—little round tables and folding chairs on the verge of collapse.

"Look at the paint and look where there's no paint." We knew what scumbling was; we knew impasto. Little by little, we saw red blotches throughout the background: van Gogh had painted this famous picture on a red-checkered tablecloth.

"Pretend you are the artist," the teacher said. "Or yourselves, grown up to be the painters I expect you to be. You're at a café. Suddenly the tables, chairs, and sky are a vision only you can see. You grab colors and brushes from the paint box you always carry with you, and paint as though your life depended on it!"

I tried to tell this story to my parents.

"Do you have any idea how much a tablecloth costs?" Daddy said. "Don't try that at the Tasty Shop, young lady."

# SOOTY WITH LOVE

In art school, I studied anatomy. I was on a first-name basis with bones. They fit together, fully interlocking, a place for even the smallest one—the world kinder then. Every morning, we drew for three hours from life, the models' bodies eloquent and lithe. During breaks, they flitted behind our easels in their moth-eaten kimonos, seeing themselves twelve different ways. I was embarrassed to look at them clothed, having held their beauty in my eyes, traced their limbs with charcoal, my fingers sooty with love. They appreciated a good likeness. They knew how to turn to the light. We learned how to *draw* light.

One day in my first year, I balled up a sketch, tossed it in the black metal wastebasket. It stared at me like a prisoner no one would visit, much less parole. Mr. Moy, the drawing teacher, plucked it out, smoothed the nude, and held her up to his glasses at various angles. Everyone watched, even the model. Models usually couldn't care less. They've seen students come and go.

"Don't you know someday you'll hang next to Rembrandt?" he scolded me. I thought he was mocking me and ran out of the room to cry in the Ladies'.

We visited the galleries filled with Abstract Expressionism—Guston, de Kooning, and Kline—every Saturday. On Sundays we went to the museums. I've kept those sketches on stained paper—studies of Rodin—the planes of men's faces still lunging off the page all these decades later. Mad about Pierre Bonnard, I painted still lifes, as though an ashtray, a basket, and a seashell contained all life. The objects isolated, suspended, about to slide off the edge.

One day at the Modern with my artist friends Greer, Robbie, and Keith, I was worshipping at the altar of Bonnard's *Breakfast Room*.

"If you love it so much," Greer said in her impudent way, "why don't you kiss it?"

We looked at each other. Robbie went down on all fours, Keith lifted me up and held me steady on Robbie's back as Greer stood by on the lookout for guards. Just when I was eye to eye with the bottom edge of the tablecloth—

"Psst!" she hissed. "Guard coming!"

I kissed the canvas between the cream pitcher and the bread. My lips touched where Bonnard's brush had been. No matter what would happen in my life, no one could take that away from me.

## BARGAIN WITH GOD

One night I was painting a tiny still life after Bonnard: basket, fruit, china on a red and white checkered cloth. Overhead in Robbie's room where my roommate Gigi was visiting, the bedsprings of love creaked and groaned. My painting's checkers faded into rose and cream, melting into each other, askew. For the first time, I had crudely achieved what Bonnard mastered with luminous grace—the sensation that the objects were falling. I cupped my hands at the bottom edge to catch them before they slipped off their shadows. The whole cloth would slide off with everything on it, like a magic trick. Without a horizon line—where are we? Below the groaning ceiling, breathing the fragrance of linseed oil and turpentine—high on the first good painting of my life—I prayed, "Dear God, let me be a real artist, and I won't ask for love."

---

In the afternoon, we painted. Our studios circled the catwalk high around Low Library's dome. Then we were ravenous art students, and apples were rubies. In one hand, the seamless ferruled brush. In the other, a long butt from the sculptured urns of cinema lobbies, ashes falling on the palette, mixing in. No time to boil water for spaghetti. Famished, we slept under our easels. I searched for three things—any three things—to put together to call a still life. Linseed oil to make it shine, varnish to make it last.

The floors of the tiny five-flight walkup Gigi and I shared on East Seventh Street slanted. For reasons of light, the easel was on the downside of the room, the palette table above. Standing on my cot with my back against the wall, I'd load the brush with color, then run down to the still life, scumble or impasto the paint, then climb back up to see the squiggly shadow of a teacup, a burnt sienna basket tipping open-mouthed, saying *Oh* on cadmium yellow and cerulean lace. As my canvases got bigger, I'd look at the painting through a reducing glass in order to see the whole picture.

## YOU DON'T HAVE TO BE JEWISH

116th St Station with Robbie and Greer. A Levy's Rye Bread poster:
*You Don't Have to Be Jewish To Love Levy's Rye Bread*—in tatters, huge ribbons of bread, hanging down like scrolls of the Torah. We grabbed handfuls as though it were real.

*Sandy Diamond*

# WHAT WAS GOING ON IN THE WORLD

One day, climbing up Low Library's wide steps, picturing a new canvas on my easel—milk bottle, teacup, rose madder flowers dancing on a cloisonné ashtray, each object tipping off its shadow on a flesh-colored chair. Wondering what John Heliker had meant the day before when his hand vaguely motioned near the picture's upper-left corner—his usual Zen critique. I was almost to the Alma Mater when I saw a huge, bearded, bear of a man in camouflage, lunging down the stairs into my path, with a swarm of men with cameras rushing after. I froze. The smiling bear grabbed my hand, pumped it, wouldn't let go, arousing the tubes of color and brushes in my paint box to thump and rattle.

The next day, several people said, "I saw you on TV, shaking hands with Castro!" I didn't know what was going on in the world.

# NEW YORK STEAK

A beau of Gigi's saw my self-portraits.

"I'll give you five bucks for that one," he said, pointing.

Even I knew it was worth more than that.

"What if I treat you to a big steak?"

I hadn't eaten in a restaurant since I'd left home. I didn't know what steaks cost in New York.

"Sure," I said, the meat already in my mouth. I thought he meant he'd take me there on a date. Instead, he scribbled down an address on a good piece of drawing paper, fished a five-dollar bill from his pocket, and left with my rolled-up face.

I found Bowery Joe's: New York Steaks Broiled Before Your Eyes. $5.

"How do you want it, girl?" the cook asked.

I wanted it impasto, burnt-umber grill marks, pink as Alizarin inside. I wanted it big enough to last 'til I got my degree. The cook slid a sizzling platter in front of me. I sat by the window, begging my teeth to slow down. On the street, everyone looked like Rembrandt's last self-portrait—austere, watchful, bankrupt.

*Sandy Diamond*

# HOW TO DRAW A COW

While I was at Columbia, I babysat a four-year-old boy whose parents were on the faculty of the New School. They kindly insisted on calling me Jonathan's governess. I loved their apartment, books, Persian rugs, and kitchen full of food the Tasty Shop never heard of.

"Help yourself to anything," they told me. They were the beautiful people one was beginning to hear about. Most of all, I loved their exquisite, mysterious son. There was a list of things I shouldn't do. Don't help him get his coat on. Let him button it himself, even if it takes an hour. Don't ever pull him—he'll rage and scare you half to death. Let him lead you. Within the hour, I was on my knees pleading.

"Jonathan, please stop screaming. I'll lose my job. I need this job, darling. I love you, Jonathan. Why can't you just say 'I'll do it myself' and forgive me before your parents get home? There's so much good food here." If only I could hold him and rock him in the rocking chair, but his parents warned me about that. We didn't have a name for autism in the fifties.

One day, crayoning, Jonathan drew a tiny recognizable cow in the bottom left corner of the paper.

When I showed this to his parents they said, "Let's take him to a farm upstate."

The next time I governed, he drew a cow that filled the whole page. "No room for the tail," Jonathan said in a rare complete sentence.

I thought to tape another sheet of paper to the back of the cow, but before I could, Jonathan put his finger on the cow's backside, and with the other hand, turned the paper over and drew a tail perfectly aligned with the body on the other side.

# FAMOUS WINTER NIGHT

One winter eve, 1958, Crazy Howie—*crazy* being a distinction, not a slur back then—whacked a stick on Gigi's and my door.

"Grab yer shabby, armynavysurplus hipster hepcat pea coats—someone wansta meetcha."

Out on the streets, blond Gigi and dark-braids me snapped past tenement-wino-storefront starving artists who couldn't stand it anymore and ate their still lifes. Genius madman Howie, who looked like the death mask of Beethoven, wouldn't say who we were going to see. Those days, everything was possible. Gods still mixed it up with mortals. Sitting on a bed in shadowy First and A, handsome as a pinup pinned to the wall of our generation, Jack Kerouac reached for me so gently, I didn't know what was coming. He lifted my braid to his lips and kissed it.

Oh, famous winter night, we trooped to another tenement—Second Street, I think it was, not knowing then I'd want to remember every detail. Up a turning stair to an unheated pad near the Hudson River, home of Allen Ginsberg, Peter Orlovsky, and Gregory Corso, the kitchen mouthwatering with a kettle of soup.

"Allen made that soup from a bone," Gregory bragged. "He went to the butcher, put on his angel face and said, 'A meaty bone, perhaps, for a bunch of angel-headed hipsters?'"

We huddled on the steamy kitchen floor, the writers reciting to each other from folded scraps of paper pried from pants pockets what they had written that day. Of course, I had read *On the Road* and *Howl*. Allen was thin, scholarly, rumpled, good-looking beyond the pictures I'd seen of him. Gregory adorable, childlike, and as wound-up as Peter Pan. The beautiful one was Peter, his face a blend of delicacy and strength. I knew he and Allen were lovers, that Allen had first seen Peter in a painting and fell in love that way. After everyone said their poems, Kerouac announced he didn't know what to wear.

The next day Kerouac would be on *The Tonight Show* for the first time with hipster Steve Allen. Shyly, Jack opened the closet door: old red and black lumberman's jacket and new black and red lumberman's jacket, at opposite ends of the hanger-dangling rod, like contestants on a quiz show.

"Whaddaya say?" smiled Jack—the last innocent night of his life, back when everyone said things for the first time. Before yesterday's paper blew down Bleecker Street—his definition of fame. I don't remember what was decided, and none of us had a TV.

Kerouac drifted away. Orlovsky left for the nightshift at Bellevue, the others calling after him, "Say hello to Carl. Say hello to…" But I didn't hear any name after Carl, no longer just a name in a poem but a real person—Carl Solomon—their beloved friend, locked up. Gigi and Gregory disappeared into his room. Howie vanished into the East River Conspiracy. I stood alone in the animal-soup-of-time kitchen with the god-who-wrote-*Howl*. Like the cheese that stands alone. But greener than cheese. Allen got into his creaky bed, held the blanket open for me. The bedsprings poked whenever I breathed, which was as little as possible. We lay together in our starving artist underwear, not touching. On an impulse, I ducked under the covers and kissed his writing elbow.

"Well, *that's* a first," he said.

*And I'd like to be a bad woman, too,*
*And wear the brave stockings of night-black lace*
*And strut down the streets with paint on my face.*
                —*Gwendolyn Brooks, "A Song in the Front Yard"*

## GIGI & MONET

I painted a large reclining nude of Gigi. Her cat, Monet, posed with her for hours at the canvas. Linseed oil smells like fish.

"Have I done her justice?" I asked Monet. I asked Gigi if Monet had ever seen her naked before.

# SALLY

Gregory visited Gigi; "visiting" meaning exuberant sex behind her thin door. He painted tiny Giottoesque angels on the edges of my canvas. Any space he could find he filled with enchanting things. I drew him in profile, a good likeness, his jumpy energy in his mischievous, peaked eyebrow, his squiggly hair. One night, Corso brought over Peter Orlovsky.

"Here's something for you," he said.

*Saint Peter*, they called him. Reviewers and friends alike called his poems *loopy*. So inexperienced, how could I have known he would be the best lover I'd ever have in my life? Fifty years later, I still remember. His smooth body, smudged with love bites from Allen, which I kissed in the hopes of thanking Ginsberg for *Howl*.

I asked Peter if he liked boys or girls better. After a long while, like he was thinking about it for the first time, and I was mad at myself that I'd asked, he said softly, "I like girls better, but I love Allen."

In the morning, Peter was typing a letter to his mother on my kitchen table. He carried his typewriter everywhere, tucked under his arm like a little brother.

"Why are you writing to her when you're here with me?"

This pouty question shows how little I knew about real writers, who need to record their experience while it's still fresh.

"I'm telling her about you," he said.

"Oh. Well, that's different." I read over his shoulder: "…a sweet lady painter name of Sally…"

"Sally! Who's Sally? Did you sneak some other girl in here while I was sleeping?"

If Peter didn't know who I was, who was I? He laughed his beatific laugh. He x'ed out *Sally* with five Xs, typed in *Sandy*. You could still make out *Sally*, looking naughtier than ever, behind her crisscross bondage veil of Xs. Whereas, my name looked provisional, secondhand.

"She better not show her face around here again! She must be some gone chick."

A voice in me said *Stop!* But I didn't listen. Peter unrolled the letter, folded it, and slipped it in his shirt pocket, patting his heart. He tucked the typewriter under his arm, still smiling. Light shed off him like halos in a religious painting, and he didn't even know how the air around him shimmered. You could imagine him in a long brown robe, carrying a little lamb. I knew he was temporary, that he'd go back to Allen. It wasn't about losing Peter. It was about losing myself.

"Is she prettier than me?"

He took the steps two at a time, walking backward, facing me, smiling at me.

"Sandy, you're Sandy," he called, so that my name echoed in the stairwell. Leaning over the rail, I watched him recede landing by landing. Everything in a crucial balance was about to tip, the difference between walking on air and falling into the abyss. Too late, I thought, "You can call me Sally. You can call me…Abigail…Prudence. You can call me anything." The last time I saw Peter was outside my chained 9th Street door, asking me to unchain the lock. Seeing his beloved face through the links reminded me of the x's on Sally's name. That's when I became someone else, someone who lost the girl I used to be.

The following week, I signed a message to Peter, *Sally*. It wasn't important to be me anymore. I wanted to go to the Five Spot, and called to see who was there. The line was busy. I needed Monk. Gramercy 7-9650. The line was still busy. I wanted Thelonious in his little red wagon, out on a limb calling,

*Coltrane! Coltrane!*

# IMPASTO & GLAZE

December of 1958. Each hour was sliding into the next. I felt I couldn't interrupt the flow. John Heliker, our painting master, said I could work at home. Columbia University's College of Painting & Sculpture had just given me a fellowship. Not just tuition but also living expenses like food and the laundromat. I could afford to move two streets further uptown to 9th Street. I was on a path.

In those days, fifteen cents bought you a subway token or a slice of good pizza. I'd flip the nickel or dime: lunch or school? My canvas still barely dry, I rode the subway up to Columbia to show Mr. Heliker. I went in the late morning to lessen the chance of anyone rubbing against the paint. On good days, I enjoyed my fellow passengers looking at the canvas, shaking their heads, then looking at me. They thought I was the end of the world. On bad days, they were muttering to each other, criticizing my colors, the brushstrokes.

On the worst days, I could bear neither being on exhibit in the subway nor the garish sight of the red and orange and yellow pizza. I could not even bear the gentle eyes of the painting master, much less my own eyes in the wild and desolate mirror. Then I'd wait for rush hour, buy a token and ride nowhere, without my art, lost in the caress of swaying subway bodies, the impasto of overcoats, the glaze of stockings, touching, touching—rocked and flung with them—singing a lullaby in my head, "I am like other people, I am like other people, I am like other people."

# NOT LIKE OTHER PEOPLE

People ask, "When exactly was your first breakdown?"

How to tell them something had sprung up inside me like mushrooms after rain, like an umbrella opening too fast and too close, an overwhelming brimmness? I painted like the Red Shoes danced—stopping was out of the question. I don't expect you to understand.

I didn't know why I was crying so much. One day in the painting studio, I tried to hide from the onslaught inside me, ran screaming to the Ladies', locked myself in a stall. Greer came after me.

"Open the latch. Slide open the latch, Sandy."

Frozen, I couldn't do it. It was as if I'd never done it before, as if no one had ever done it before. Finally, she crawled under the door, dragged me out along the marble floor, and held on to me as we descended all the steps past the *Alma Mater*'s upstretched arms, her scepter, her crown, her wisdom, and made our way toward the subways. I watched as her hand, splattered with Titanium White, gripped my coat, steered me through the hospital's sliding door. Then we were in the ER, and I heard a nurse tell Greer a doctor was coming for me, that I was safe, and she could go. Greer hugged me goodbye.

The emergency room was empty. Instead of chairs, there were benches as in a train station or a church. It felt like something important would happen there. I'd be transported or a spirit would change me. I was departing from where I had been. I got very quiet and listened. Behind a curtained alcove just beyond the oxygen tanks, white-uniformed nurses and aides drank Cokes, murmured, and smoked.

The skeletal arms of the clock pulsed, then lurched as though trying to get away from the scene. Or each other. An hour passed. Every time the minute hand groped its way to the next numeral—as though it had never done this before, unsure of the way. The doctor never came. I was there for ninety goddamned minutes on the interminable clock, and no doctor came. I sidled out the ER door, ready to run if anyone tried to stop me. No one looked up.

# RILKE IN THE VILLAGE

Outside, it was the Village, MacDougal Street. The cigarette butts on the pavement had lipstick kissed on them, the color of my mother's lipstick. I chose the longest one. The trash bins were nicer here than the ones uptown, and as I fished out sticks of wood to feed my potbellied stove, I heard a man say in a German accent,

"May I be of assistance?"

The speaker was old, his voice like Rilke's reading from *The Duino Elegies*. The next thing I knew, we had our arms full of sticks, and then we were in his study in huge leather armchairs, which I feared and felt embraced by and which dwarfed me so that my feet didn't touch the floor, and he said his name was Martin, once the head of Philosophy at the University of Salzburg until he had to flee. And then Rilke sang to me through Martin:

*Ask no one to speak of you, even contemptuously, and when you hear your name on the lips of men, take it no more seriously than anything else from those lips. Take another name, any other, so that God may call you in the night. So that God may call you in the night.*

# ALTERATIONS

Later, Martin must have walked me to my storefront. I'd whitened the windows with lime for privacy and light as the real painters did. I reveled in this invisibility. No one passing on 9th Street could see me spying on them through a crack in the paint. When did it occur to me that I could barely see out? I heard footsteps as people carried boots with worn soles to the shoe repair shop, a lady's high-buttoned shoe trembling on the sign's hinge. Or a threadbare coat to the tailor—*fix me, make me better*—a second smaller sign creaking on its hinge, *Seamstress*, promising *Alterations*. I held my breath past the Hungarian bakery—its faded fruit pie sign, steam rising from the latticed crust, its fragrance chasing after me, no money for a bun.

I heard someone outside calling my name. I squinted through a crack in the lime, saw blackness. Barricaded in my storefront—chair tipped under the doorknob as I'd seen besieged men do in movies. A crazy pounding—my heart or someone at the door?

"Sandy. I know you're in there. Open the door or I'll chop it down. I have an axe."

The calm voice of my friend Stan. Stan the Rescuer who'd already graduated from Princeton. Not raggedy like the rest of us: a tweed sports jacket, suede elbow patches.

Stan was the one of us who didn't go crazy.

"When did you eat last?" he asked through the keyhole. "Let's go to Ratner's, kiddo, and eat something—whatever you want." *Kiddo*, like Daddy. Or was it Daddy, not Stan at all? Daddy would tempt me with delicatessen this way.

I yanked away the barricade. Tall Stan filled the space where the door had been. He stuffed me gently into my peacoat and held on to its sleeve all the way to Ratner's.

*What shall I do? What shall I do? Now low, a murmur, now precise as the headwaiter's: And to follow?*
—Samuel Beckett, *I Can't Go On, I'll Go On*

# THE SIZE OF A PICKLE

The din, the glaring light. I jumped when the waiter—cadaverous in a black suit and haughty as the czar—thrust a huge menu the size of Russia in my face. I couldn't see Stan, who took over.

"She'll have the Reuben. Tongue on an onion roll for me."

Even at the Tasty Shop, I always wondered if the tongue could taste you back.

The waiter flourished a chewed-up pencil in the pungent air. Perhaps he communicated with the kitchen via sky-writing. He whisked the menus from our hands and skated away as though in a former life he had been in the Ice Capades. "He hates me," I whispered to Stan.

"I doubt that," Stan said. "Being haughty is a job requirement at Ratner's."

He shook the folds from our white cloth napkins, tucked one on my lap, as though I could have forgotten how to do this—me, the deli owner's daughter. The waiter reappeared, sliding our huge plates on the table, just out of reach. I realized how hungry I was, had been for days. But something was wrong.

"Pickle too small," I murmured to Stan. "The pickle must be commensurate with the sandwich."

"Oh, what have we got here," the waiter sneered, "an Einstein?"

"Look, my good man," Stan said, "kindly bring us another pickle." *My good man*—that must be how they talk at Princeton.

"Not two little pickles," I cried. "One *big* pickle." Why can't people understand me?

Stan reached across the table and raised my plate toward the waiter. "Please bring this plate back with a single big pickle. A really. Big. Pickle."

The waiter stood as though posing for a statue of all that's insufferable about America. He clutched a napkin between both hands, ready to blindfold or strangle someone.

Through clenched teeth, he said, "Ratner's. Makes. The Best. Pickles. In New York."

"I agree, I agree," said Stan. "You are absolutely right. However, this skinny little pickle is unacceptable in this context, *per se*."

The two men stared at each other.

Stan said in a friendly voice, "What is your name, sir, if I may ask?"

"Adolf!" The waiter grabbed my plate and vanished.

"He's a Nazi," I whispered to Stan. "He knows we're Jews."

"Everyone here is Jewish. It's a Jewish deli. They wouldn't hire a Nazi. He had that name before—you know…before."

"He should have changed his name," I hissed.

In no time, Adolf was back. Crowding the sandwich half off the plate was a pickle the size of a cucumber. Stan was beaming. I lifted the sandwich to my mouth. A big chunk of wet sauerkraut fell out. I started to cry. Stan slid me from my chair to his lap, cut the sandwich in quarters. His arms around me, he fed me.

"Eat," he said in his beautiful voice. "Eat now. You are safe."

---

Now, people say Ratner's didn't serve meat. Yet I know this happened. I remember it. I remember my despair when the sauerkraut slid out, remember opening my mouth for the next bite while Stan held me on his lap, one napkin covering both our knees. I may have been going crazy but I still knew pastrami from a blintz.

Back on the street, there was a telephone booth. Stan called my parents.

# A POT BIG ENOUGH TO PUT A NAUGHTY CHILD INTO

Up broad stairs from the Tasty Shop dining room—Michael and I climbed to the bakeshop. Studded silver ovens and giant pots big enough to put a naughty child into, gleaming bins of flour dwarfed even Sy the baker's white clothes and poofy crowned hat. Not even Daddy had a hat like that. Sy was the king of the Upper Tasty Shop, the only employee with permission to spank us if we were bad. Once, Michael yanked my braid as I flew past on the pastry floor and dipped it in a vat of dough. When Sy turned my brother over his knee, a Biblical cloud of retribution rose from the crime scene, to my delight.

Sy glided among hot apple pies rising, fruit bubbling from golden crusts, the tables powdered with flour. We ran through strudel and cheesecake, tarts and rye, challah braided like Mother's hair, past vats of poppyseeds, sesame, cherries, and glaze.

Now and then, in dark years ahead when life smelled of defeat, I'd get a whiff of the bakeshop, a glimpse of Sy gliding through loaves and pie, an artist at one with his heaven.

# THE BRACELET

I remember speaking to a bracelet laying in the gutter in front of my door. A heart-shaped charm on a broken chain. Amazing no one else had found it first—usually in that neighborhood, the gutters were picked clean. No, it was meant for me. Once I picked it up, we were inseparable. In my pocket, the mangled heart told my thigh its story. It was, as you'd expect, the usual boy-meets-girl affair. He gave her the bracelet, then broke her heart. She threw it from a speeding car. Most of all, the bracelet grieved because the same hand that had caressed it tore open the latch and flung it without warning to the pavement. It had done nothing to deserve this.

Under the cloth, my thigh ached for the bracelet. I moved it to the other pocket. The ache spread through my body. Finally I put it on the table, where it cried. It mourned from the shelf. Whatever I did, the whole room throbbed from its metallic heartache. I tied it to my wrist but I felt weighed down. At bedtime I began to untie the string. The bracelet informed me its real girl slept with it on. I tried not to think this to spare the bracelet's feelings, but between the time it had hit the street and I had found it, it had been run over—the ragged links bitten by all the sharp teeth of Manhattan, the heart unrecognizable.

At this point, my parents flew in. Both of them. From Ohio to New York. They had a business to run. I don't know how they did it. My parents were sticklers about dressing nice. I let Mother change my clothes, but the bracelet had to stay. They brought me up right, taught me how to dress, how to behave in public. They took me to a shrink on Park Avenue. Fifty dollars an hour in 1959. They didn't have money to throw away—if I learned anything from them, I learned that. And they threw it away on him.

"Tell me about your bracelet," he said.

So I did. That's how cooperative I was. And you know what he did? He told my parents their daughter would never live outside an institution.

How do I know he said that? My mother must have told my aunt, and my aunt told me—that's how things got communicated in my family. Not then—she would have told me later, after the hospital, when I was about to go back to New York. She wanted me to know I'd proved him wrong. When she said it, I remembered the bracelet. What had happened to it? Somewhere along the line, they got it away from me. To them, it was the enemy. They would have thrown it away. Again. Once it was shiny in a glass showcase. Perhaps it had a velvet box. Everyone admired it, pointing. The boy chose it above all the other pieces of jewelry. He paid good money. To the clerk he would have said, "That's for my girl."

# DON'T JUMP

For those of you who don't know what manic means, whose friends never flew out their upper-story bedroom window, flapping their arms. Manic, my friends, is when you're all acceleration and no brakes, when you can't leave your paintings so you lower a basket on a rope out the fifth-floor window down to the street—leaning out—where your roommate fills it with orange juice and Hershey bars, all you've eaten for weeks, aware enough to read *HER* and *SHE* in the chocolate. While you pull up the rope—the basket heavier now, your arms trembling—the neighborhood kids yell, "Don't jump, lady!" How could they know you *don't* jump when you're manic? When you're manic, you fly.

# THE DARKEST TIME

The darkest time I had the pills to end the farce. Instead of taking them all at once, I took them one by one. I don't know why. My first fling with madness. This was before friends passed pills around like Jujubes. This was the first time, when I had nothing to compare it to.

Whenever I woke up, there was another pill, although fewer than before. Did I think—hearing footfalls (each softer than the last) on the sidewalk receding—that Mother was coming to save me, my mother with a bunch of violets from our Ohio woods? Could all the innocence of childhood—story time, lap, puppies, baseball—find me here behind the opaque glass in a room hung with still lifes? (The violets wouldn't be out yet.)

Lying on my cot, I faced my last painting—a torn loaf of bread and a sugar bowl on a striped cloth. *My poor painting*, I thought, *I am leaving you*. And awakened again to its jagged brushstrokes like fingers. By the third day, I saw I couldn't leave the painting unfinished. Let someone else finish it, I told God. But who was I kidding? It wasn't a matter of choice. I was assigned to do it. Instead of death, I had the still life. And besides, the pills were gone.

*It took a few years, then I finished the painting. I wish I could show it to you. Even though it saved my life, I underestimated its value. I sold it—I needed the money, but now I want it back again, just to see if I remember it right, to see if it was worth living for.*

What friend packed up my canvases, brushes, and paint, the ashtrays, seashells, the blue cloisonné box, smiling with red flowers? The shell with parted lips and the shell without a mouth, coiled into itself—irreplaceable, all of it! I paint still lifes—where are they, where are they, what if I could have still had that life?

Depression—but this was the first time—it had no name yet—irrevocable as tides, holds you in the heavy arms of the heaving sea, shuts your eyes with speckled shells, floods your mouth with brine. Nine months, opaque and moonless. Stars are out of the question. The only thing the disease tells you is the dazzling will never come again.

Sandy Diamond

# KEROUAC IN THE ASYLUM

A poet, years later, asked me if Kerouac had kissed the right braid or the left. It was December 1958—I knew that much because I wrote it down. By February, I'd be in my first asylum, in my lunatic's cot, where they wanted to know why I had broken the neck of a turpentine bottle, daring the walls to come any closer. In the asylum of zombie injections, they wanted to know why I had a knife collection and tried to burn the house down. No, that was later. It hadn't happened yet. That couldn't have been me they were talking about. No, that wasn't then, not yet, that was later, much later—a different time for the fire, the knife, the gun. Now—this was the first time. I was on a narrow rack. Kerouac jacked me up through the quicksand jaws of Thorazine.

> *I am too feeble to go on, says the Wizard in the Castle bending over his papers at night. "Faustus!" cries his wife from the bath… "Stop fiddling with your desk papers and pen quills in the middle of the night, come to bed, the mist is on the air of night lamps, a dew'll come to rest your fevered brow at morning—you'll lie swaddled in sweet sleep like a lambikin—I'll hold you in my old snow-white arms—and all you do is sit there dreaming.*
>
> —*Jack Kerouac, Doctor Sax*

"Snap out of it," said Father. Mother's rat-tailed comb carving childhood's part down the center of my skull in my rat's nest hair—oh, poetry hair in Peter's hands—and the nurse snapped, "Cut it, why don't we? Why don't we just cut it right off?"

As cowed as my parents were by the medical profession, even they knew I wouldn't be me without my long hair. Kerouac lifted my braid between

First and A. He kissed it. I'm not making this up. I have witnesses. Did he know I was about to lose my only mind?

*Recently on the radio, I heard Henry Louis Gates—Harvard Chair of African American Studies—say how it felt when he first went to Africa: a black man in a black continent, everyone like him for the first time in his life. He compared it to how he imagined an American Jew would feel visiting Israel. And I thought, Yes! That's how I felt when I was mad in the madhouse. At last, not having to pretend to be like normal folks. The catatonics, the schizies, the paranoids—these were my people. We could be crazy to our heart's content—it was expected of us. Now we could play triple solitaire or ping-pong all day long. Or stare into space. Or have an episode.*

# DR. CALIGARI

I first saw Dr. Weiss in a storeroom at Mount Sinai Hospital, Cleveland. *Restore me.* There wasn't a bed for my sudden arrival in the loony bin. Chairs, cabinets, even tables were piled on top of each other, so pushed-together we had to burrow to make room for our feet. Did they think they could cure me in this setting of jagged props, this *Cabinet of Dr. Caligari*? I hadn't talked or looked at anyone for days. No one could touch my clothes or hair. Gradually I realized the doctor's shoes (just like my father's shoes—spectators with tiny holes for the feet to see where they're going) were wedged and twisted like mine. He was speaking. I was faraway. His voice reached me in increments—tender without babying, believable without scaring me. Later when I knew what a reverb mic was, that's how he sounded—deep and slow and with an echo. I fell into a well of surrender. I felt safe with the furniture every which way. I told him my story. It lasted eight years.

# HOW THE WORLD LOOKED

In the psych ward, we had two teenagers, both depressed. I prefer manic myself, but we take what we can get. They were moping around like regular teenagers, only clinically. Once, in the dayroom, the girl slouched over the jigsaw puzzle that was always in progress and never finished. Some idyllic scene from the outside world, full of holes. Her short, blond hair fell over her face. I wondered if her family would keep her well-groomed in the locked ward or were they the kind that eventually figures, *Why bother? No one sees her anyway.*

I'd done this puzzle a million times—snowcapped mountains reflected in a lake. This puzzle is planted in every mental institution in America so we'll reflect on why we're here, while our parents—in the real world, haha—look high and low for an insurance policy with a clause for Nervous Breakdown. In the water, the white snow and the blue mountains looked like those pictures of Earth seen from space. The time I'm talking about was before that perspective, but I am looking back now. I am reflecting. The Declaration of Independence

The only puzzle we had during The War when we couldn't get new jigsaw puzzles, my father and I did The Signing of the Declaration of Independence a thousand times. At the beginning of The War, I was learning to print letters in sticks and hoops. On V-Day, our school marched along Chagrin River Road, banging on pots and pans. By then we'd learned cursive where the sticks hit the hoops, making the letters slant.

The whole alphabet had to hold hands to keep from falling.

When Daddy raised the lid from the puzzle box, the puzzle pieces lay scattered or in clumps, like soldiers who had lost their limbs. A thousand times, I connected the bits of John Hancock's signature.

"Mr. Hancock signed so big," Daddy said, "not because he was a show-off like you, but to show the British he wasn't afraid of them."

Then we'd fit together all the quills of all the Founding Fathers.

"A quill's a strong feather from the wing of a goose," Daddy said every time the last piece fit.

After four years of this, you think about America in a way unknown to people who don't do jigsaw puzzles.

---

As if there were a penalty for being wrong, the girl in the psych ward tried a piece timidly, instead of jamming it in and pretending it fit, like a manic would. Boy teen appeared out of nowhere, swept the table with his arm. A few pieces clung to each other as they fell. The blue eye of the lake wept on the dayroom floor. The girl stared at the sudden emptiness before her. He scooped the fractured mountains from the floor, dumped handfuls back on the table. Eyes down, they turned all the pieces color side up. Their eyes met. Better than Librium.

After that, they were inseparable, interlocking. Imagine love in that place, everyone watching. When the medication hit the bloodstream, the nervous system, he'd press a piece hard even after the fit was secure, and she'd lightly tap the same piece, and he'd find that adorable instead of going crazy as someone not in love might have done. The puzzle was their intermediary. They'd pick up a piece, its configurations like sex. When they held hands, their plastic inmate wristbands rubbed in a way that made me turn away to cry. You couldn't tell them from sweethearts in the real world. I was twenty-two, I'd blown my chances.

# THE QUESTIONER

"So their troubles were over."

Who said that? There was a voice in Mount Sinai with me, separate from explainable sounds. What did it want from me? Was The Questioner Dr. Weiss? I decided to humor it.

"Actually, no. Their troubles were just beginning."

"What makes you say that?" This is the psychiatric technique in a nutshell.

"They got discharged. The families are warned not to let their ex-patient have contact with another former patient. As you well know. She was re-admitted with bandages on her wrists. She couldn't even do a puzzle anymore."

"Now, just a minute!" The Questioner interrupted me. "The puzzle girl? I'm in charge of this ward. If this happened, I'd be the first to know. Is this Let's Pretend?

"Okay, let's say all this happened and my staff hid it from me. Still, I don't believe the only two teenagers on the ward would fall in love. Sandy, you should admit you're making it up."

"Okay, I lied about the girl. *He* was real. I wanted to give him someone to love."

"Jamming in the puzzle pieces—you were talking about yourself."

*2003: On the radio, the interviewer asked Alice Walker if one of her characters was autobiographical. She said, "In my work, the tables and the lamps are me."*

Fifty-some years later, I wish I could have quoted that to Dr. Weiss, but by then I was passing for normal, and he was dead. The Questioner had got himself in my head. Let me be him, seeing me. Then we'd know how to fix me. Right?

*Sandy Diamond*

## ONCE I WAS A RABBIT

Real enough to fool a hunter. Every fall, in the field beyond the blackberries, the hunters' red and black caps stalked in the high grass. A Crayola black rifle in the sky where Mother said geese had a perfect right to be. A bang, a puff where the duck had been. When Michael and I were four and five, we hopped and ran and crumpled to the ground, playing Rabbits. One day, a bullet whizzed past me and nicked the back edge of the porch, then flew into the woods. I saw the whorls of Daddy's thumb as he felt the splintered shingle.

"Coulda been anything," he said. "I mighta nicked it with the mower."

The woods so big, a bullet so small.

# BUICK, CADILLAC

Which breakdown did this precede? They all started the same way—painting, no time to clean the palette, squeezing new paint on the still-wet old, color on the drawer pulls, inside the drawers, saucers, dinner plates, the salad bowl; so, everything tasted of Mars Violet and Viridian.

Who called my parents this time? They got wind of my drift; they drove to New York to check up on me. I bathed and dressed, brushed my long ropes of hair. I still knew how to be a looker. We went to lunch, a Broadway show—*Hair*. Oh, incendiary soul, I sat still and didn't yell "Fire!" And then it was over.

At the parking garage, the attendant opened the Buick door for Mother. When cars have names, not people—that's what madness is.

"Goodbye. Goodbye." Blowing kisses, they were gone, taking with them my lacquer of sanity.

"Was that your mother?" the attendant said. "What a beautiful woman. Let me show you my fine cars. Look at this Caddy, feel that upholstery."

Fucking in the back seat, was that me? My parents already on the freeway asking each other, "Didn't she look good?"

And then I was safe—almost safe, somewhat safe—I thought I was safe, but perhaps the meaning of the word *safe* had changed while I was busy losing my mind. What friend next time would say, "Let's call your parents"?

"They were just here!" I'd cry. "They're still on their way home!" Not knowing how many days had passed.

# SECOND GRADE

When I was in second grade, all the real teachers went to work in the wartime factories. The district sent us a teacher fresh out of teacher school named Miss Thornbush. We became foes in October when the class said my Halloween cat looked scarier than hers, and she wouldn't pin mine up on the board.

I told stories to my classmates during lunch—usually peanut butter and jelly on Wonder Bread. After lunch, we were supposed to go outside and play Red Rover or marbles or hopscotch or—our favorite—Cowcatcher. But no one left the lunch table, they wanted to hear the end of the story. The teacher must have warned me to stop talking so much. I don't remember that part, if true. All I know is one day, in the cafeteria, she held my arm and taped stiff cardboard blinders by my eyes. She told the other kids not to talk to me and to get lots of exercise during recess. My mother must have agreed with this punishment, packing only an apple and half a sandwich so I would finish eating faster.

# BREAKDOWN

My first nervous breakdown was in 1959. Now it was 1960 and it was happening again. Only time would tell if this was to be an annual event, something we could mark on the calendar. "February: Sandy—manic or depressed?" In the margin, the doctor's phone number.

A while back I asked my sister, Dianne, if she remembered any of this.

"I remember whenever the family sat down to dinner," she said, "the phone rang, and Mom and Dad jumped up and ran upstairs, and before I even knew, came down with a suitcase and said, 'Sandy needs us. Aunt Ruth is coming. Be good. Finish your lamb chop.' I felt like it was always happening for years and years, and I hated you."

At some point, there was a family conference with Dr. Weiss. I remember my father saying to the doctor, "Maybe you don't know this, but I went to art school. Some oil paints are poisonous. They contain cobalt, arsenic, copper, lead! The fumes affect the brain, Doctor. I just want you to take that into account."

Mother touched his arm and murmured, "Sam, if that were true, all painters would be mad."

# VISITING HOUR

You can smell the fear. It reeks of grade-school mucilage. It's seeped into the walls, mixing with our delicious fear of Miss Thornbush catching us with paste on our lips. You can taste the shame. The parents put on a happy face, the face we couldn't manage at home. We don't have to hold that dime-store mask in front of our real faces here, for fear the elastic will snap. The parents talk to their inmates in baby talk:

"Did Sonny have a nice dinner? Did he eat it all up?" Once a mother even said "din-din." The guy was forty. Was I the only one who wanted to kill her? Parents are just like us—they don't know what to do. Baby talk, I suppose, takes them back to when they had some control over their child. But we've moved on to a new tableau, a diorama of the deranged. Wait—how can that be? Diorama is all about arrangement. Well, it isn't easy, going mad. You have to have a knack for it. You have to be born for it. The very Daddy who says, "Snap out of it" is the one who gave you the gene for madness. Haha! How do you like *that*? Okay, we didn't know it at the time. Mommy and Daddy didn't know. Hey, the doctors didn't know.

Now that we do know, how much is retroactive? Where is the retribution for my parents' grief? How much do I get for every friend who crossed the street to avoid me, my dearest friend who shut the door in my face? What consolation prize for the lovers who tried to stay in love with me? No one fucking knew. But now. Now we know. It's a gene. It's not our fault.

## MONTEMARTRE

Outside his asylum window, Utrillo painted Montmartre. Posters of these colorful oils once adorned the cinder-block walls of college dorms, and you can still see them at travel agencies, advertising Paris. Would Utrillo laugh? Or cry? Or scream? The French know how to treat a mad artist. We see quaint landscapes, but Utrillo painted his frustration; his street narrows almost to its vanishing point—a church, fence, or wall, always blocks any way to the horizon. He sketched views of Notre Dame outside his asylum window. Trees' bare branches shroud the cathedral where Quasimodo flung his stunted body in ecstasy and despair.

## DR. JEKYLL & MR. HYDE

I knew from migraines the sensation of trying to get away from my own head. *The Strange Case of Dr. Jekyll and Mr. Hyde*, the connection merely a matter of time until those *polar twins…continuously struggling*, proved to be me. Of course, a manic-depressive doesn't need to mix a tincture or quaff *some volatile ether* to switch identities. We have our own internal chemistry, our own *profound duplicity of life*. Poor Jekyll, laboring under a blackness of distress no fancy can exaggerate. Poor, poor Hyde:

*…a heady recklessness…a dissolution of the bonds of obligation. I knew myself…to be more wicked, tenfold more wicked…and the thought braced and delighted me like wine.*

# RILKE IN OHIO

Between breakdowns, I returned to Ohio. Our family home was twenty miles outside of Cleveland. The trees looked like paintings of trees. In April and May, cherry blossoms bloomed on the hillsides. My dad and his friends built a Cape Cod house he had ordered from a Sears and Roebuck catalog.

Now I wish I could go back to ask my parents how they felt when they found the first brown-paper-wrapped book in our mailbox without postage, address, or return address. Just my name: *Sandy*. In blue-black ink, a foreign hand—no American was taught to cross t's in a long upward slant, making a pattern of flying. The first book was *Sonnets to Orpheus*. It was inscribed:

*To Sandy, whose brooding and luminous magnificence of soul redeems this world thru the creation and preservation of the things of the Spirit and of Beauty.*
—*Martin, April 1959*

What—my parents must have wondered—did this Martin have to do to get this book to our mailbox in person? Was he actually here? Had he flown in from New York, and somehow found our address?

A second package arrived in May: *Translations from the Poetry of Rainer Maria Rilke*.

*To Sandy, whose aspirations are more glorious than the splendor of all astral constellations.*
—*Martin*

I couldn't remember what Martin and I talked about. No memory of what would have given him such an extreme opinion of me or himself. I remembered an old man with white hair, a short beard, and the German accent. A book-lined room. Was there a fireplace, a fire? Was the bundle of scrap wood we'd gathered waiting on a Persian rug between us, glad to be out of the cold? He must have served tea in a cup of delicate European china, painted with tiny hand-painted flowers, rimmed in gold. But perhaps when he left Germany there wasn't time to pack up the china. Perhaps my hands were shaking too much to lift the cup that may not even have been there—exquisite or chipped—to my chapped lips.

We must have talked of Rilke. My only Rilke book then was a battered paperback of *The Notebooks of Malte Laurids Brigge* a friend had given me. Pages marked with lightly penciled lines. I am still afraid to deface a book, more afraid to forget what once meant so much to me. Rilke spoke of a loneliness, an isolation, and an ecstasy I didn't have words for. My favorite passage is when in his room in a small hotel in Paris, Malte senses through the wall his neighbor's despair.

*I had my own life, and the life next door was quite another life with which I shared nothing: the life of a medical student who was studying for his examination. I listened so that my heart grew loud. I hit upon the idea of offering him my own will. I stood on my side of the wall and begged him to help himself to my will. And in time it became clear to me that he was accepting it.*

Then for the first time, Malte hears someone entering his neighbor's room.

*All was still as when some pain ceases, as if a wound were healing...My God, I thought, his mother is there. She was sitting beside the lamp, talking to him, perhaps he had leaned his head a little against her shoulder. In a minute she would be putting him to bed.*

This is why I loved Rilke. Instead of certitude, he writes *maybe, perhaps, it is possible*. He said *perhaps*, and made it happen for us. He imagines his neighbor with a mother. How often in New York I wanted my mother to save me. Put me to bed. But I was too proud. Until my hands were full of craziness and I'd forgotten how to open my fingers, see my lifeline, didn't know how to put the craziness down and pick up sanity.

When our mail was delivered, my parents were always at the Tasty Shop. With a mix of dread and longing, it was up to me to watch for the mailman. Then to watch for Martin at the end of the drive. It was June.

*To An Insane Degree*

Mother's peonies—crimson, red, white, two shades of pink—sumptuous in their borders. Climbing roses adorned arched trellises just as in past years before I was crazy. Daydreaming, I didn't see when the last brown-papered book was slipped into the mailbox. *The Duino Elegies*. All three books were first editions, Norton: 1938, '39, and '42. The deckled edges ruffled in my hands like frosting. This time. there was a frontispiece, a black-and-white photograph of Picasso's *Saltimbanques*:

*To Sandy, The cold fire of a gem burning in the void of my being.*
— *Martin*

This sounded like a lover. He'd gone too far. He must have loved someone in another life who was these superlative things. I must have reminded him of her. Martin, your language frightened me. My parents thought you were mad. Where did you go in between delivering the books? Did you stay in Cleveland at a hotel? Or return to New York and fly back again?

Martin, when I returned to New York, did I try to find you? I was on my first year of Thorazine—the first of ten years meant to keep me out of the hospital, on an even keel. At the price of memory. Did I try to find you and fail? Or were you no longer where you had been? And if I didn't try, Martin, forgive me.

*Sandy Diamond*

# THE COPS: GATES MILLS, 1960

Reminiscing about the family affliction with my sister some years back, I said, "Well, at least they never called the cops on me."

"But they did call the cops," she said. "It was winter. I remember because you were waving a gun around and yelling, 'Get Dianne out of here,' then they called Aunt Ruth to come for me, and then they called the cops. "You were holed up in the dining room," she said, and that's when I recalled the dark jungle wallpaper from the fifties' remodel that I blame for all my fear of change—the slashed green flesh of philodendron and anthurium's red poker, splashed on all four walls to an insane degree. The jungle was between the breakfast room and the hall. I barricaded myself in, forgetting that the door to the breakfast room was a swinging door. The cops opened it inch by inch with their naked fingers and peered at me, their shiny buckles glancing off the mirrored push plate. The gun would have been grabbed from my brother's collection. Was it loaded? Did the cops have their guns out? Was I taken to the hospital? There couldn't have been too many manic episodes in our small town. Dianne told me she cried all the way to Aunt Ruth's, half an hour away. As they left, I remember the officers apologizing to Mother for tracking in the snow.

# COFFIN & BLOOD

No beds at Mount Sinai. Cleveland's other mental hospital was Ingleside, a fortress on Euclid Avenue. What would Euclid have thought of its dank cells inhabited by the least logical people in the Greater Cleveland area? Withered, aspen, and frail, the attendants Miss Coffin and Mrs. Blood skirt the drafty asylum corridor, we patients in their wake ashuffle—careful lest the clammy wall tap us on the shoulder—their medieval knot of keys chattering in the damp. Keys, *tra-la*, as though they were showing us the way to something that would explain the unknown. As though one of those keys or a combination of keys could release the bolt of rage locked within us.

I was allowed to draw with a pointed pencil. "Sharper, sharper!" I cried. It was always Miss Coffin who sharpened my pencil. The dryer tasks fell naturally to her. I had learned to make a pencil point in first grade, possibly kindergarten. I was apparently too dangerous to perform this act now. On the outside, we thought nothing of thrusting a pencil into the aperture, turning the handle while the lead grew sleek. The whiff of shaven wood curls recalling Daddy, whittling clothespin dollies long ago.

# PEGGY & BUZZY

In Occupational Therapy, Miss Coffin and Mrs. Blood propped up catatonic Peggy in a brown chair. Lumpy in a crumpled housedress, Peggy's arms were too big for the spindly arms of the chair. Her legs stayed where Coffin or Blood crossed them, a position of which most people would soon tire.

"Peggy," I whispered, "may I draw you?" Her face didn't change so I felt I had her permission. I could count on Peggy sitting still. Her feet in clodhopper mules too big for the paper. She wasn't going anywhere. Unlike some people who—enemies of art—realize you're drawing them, and move on purpose or get up and walk away.

Behind Peggy was a window, barred, of course. The limbs of a naked tree branched out of her head. Loathsome February. Silent, immobile, indifferent. Still, I believed she looked forward to my visits. She was put away, put away, put away.

Leaving out the window bars, I drew the Tudor house next door, its trim crisscrossing like winter's branches and Peggy's legs. I loved Peggy. She was me if I gave up.

I drew nurses, my fellow inmates, the houseplants at the nurses' station. In freedom, I used to draw my own face, but refused to look in institutional mirrors bolted to the bathroom wall.

One day in Occupational Therapy, I drew a picture of Buzzy, a teenaged mathematical genius. Or so I was told. He was making a basket. If anyone could do it, it was him. Most of us couldn't master the potholder. In my drawing, the unwoven straw slashed upward across his face, his fingers a mass of squiggles, his brush-cut pencil jabs on top of his head. Knit brow, cleft chin. Mouth parted in concentration, knuckles a perfect clamshell. He grew out of the unfinished basket.

# HOW TO DRAW A NURSE

Three nurses in a row in the dayroom. The sketch I made of them dated February 20, 1960. One nurse in a stuffed armchair falls off the left edge of the page. She has no face. Large and white, the middle figure clasps her arms under her bosom and turns toward the third nurse, who looks at me with defiant eyebrows, faint eyes, and no mouth. Her hands hold onto her chair as though if I don't stop staring at her, she's going to get up any minute and slap my face. This is the nurse who lost her job because of my drawing.

My pencil saw more than my eyes, more than anyone's eyes, until they saw the drawing. The folds of her uniform rode high under her breasts and low on her lap, leaving the expanse in between looking like pregnancy. You're not allowed to be pregnant on staff in a mental hospital. Everyone knows that. She'd been hiding it. When I showed the drawing—for me, a triumph of organization, my only hospital art with more than one isolated figure—staff and inmates knew immediately what that spacious belly meant. And the parted legs.

Was she kind, impatient, mean? I look at her now on this smudged page, pencil lines jagged and serene. Now I wonder how she could have gotten another job. I hope you had a fine baby, ma'am. And enough to feed it. Back then—at the time—I crowed, "I'm an artist! I'm still an artist!" I was a real artist in the loony bin. Everyone knew it. I was Utrillo.

*Sandy Diamond*

# DON'T CROWD A MANIC

In the mental ward between visiting days, smoke call was our link to home. Smokers were the only thing we were that they weren't trying to change. Of course it was the family that stuck you in there in the first place, but lunatics are forgiving if only Dad remembers their brand. How long can you coddle the ash before it falls, either that or tap with every puff whether it needs it or not, depending on your personality disorder. I was in the long-ash camp. Some days how long the ash would last was the only thing I could control.

Once in the smoke line, an aide tried to give a Marlboro to a Camel smoker. Unable to convince the authorities of the mix-up, the man wept and raged until the final arbiter—a straitjacket—was applied. The rest of us determined not to read the writing on whatever was handed us. Later, out of sight of staff, we traded until everyone got their brand. Those were the best cigarettes of all.

I admit I was manic—how could I pretend otherwise? That's why I was there. They should have known. But no, they came at night with their vicious party of pills in soufflé cups meant to hold coleslaw or extra olives, filled instead with the sleek pits of sedation. And the quivering paper cup of water. I did try to take the pills, whatever lies they told afterward. Who wouldn't choke and gag, the capsules long as eels? When I wasn't swallowing fast enough to suit them, they crowded in like sharks. Everyone knows you don't crowd a manic. This was a private hospital. My parents were paying good money. I threw the paper cup of water smack in the face of the head nurse. There was an *oh*, and a falling back, and then she punched me in the face, and then there was a holding of us apart, and then my face swelled up so I couldn't see, and the next visiting day, they didn't let my parents come. And the next time in the smoke line, there was no smoke for me.

"You shouldn't smoke anyway," said the scum who couldn't tell a Camel from a Marlboro, "with your mouth like that," waving me out of line. Through the slits of my eyes, I saw my comrades approach in a haze, their lit cigarettes in their outstretched hands. In a way, I smoked them all. In a way, I smoke them still.

Moments after the nurse hit me, my leg went numb. I crumpled, was carried to my cot. A real doctor—not a shrink—pulled off my pants, my leg swollen from thigh to toe, circulation cut off from the panties' elastic, which he cut. Pain flooded the leg. I got dreamy painkillers and a vintage rattan wheelchair. *Ben-Hur* was just out that year. Inexplicably, staff allowed the inmates to take turns pushing my chair up and down the hall so fast my hair lifted its oily clumps and flew out from my itchy head. Aides and nurses lined the walls, grinning like banshees. The doctor said it was hysterical gout.

"Ben-Hur!" we screamed.

# AUNT ROSE

If your heart's on the blink, they take your family history. But if your mind is playing tricks on you, no one in the fifties asked about the strange malady of Aunt Rose, thrice-divorced.

She stayed with us once when I was eight. The family was taking turns. A ruff of electrocuted hair, a gravelly voice. A face, Mother said, like a lion. The worst thing: a chain smoker—Chesterfields, the pack illustrated with golden castles and minarets. Aunt Rose was the oldest girl of my father's eight siblings—Max, Jack, Rose, Faye, Oscar, Benny, Leo, and Sam. Rose got the full blast of the family curse. My informant from my mother's side told me Aunt Faye was aloof and glamorous. She forbade us kids to call her *Aunt*—sent herself long-stemmed red roses from a secret admirer no one ever met.

When Aunt Rose was happy, she ran up and down Carnegie Avenue, buying every dress in sight. My mother said so. I could hear Mother all the way from the kitchen, telling my father he'd better know how to get the smell of smoke out of the couch where his sister had parked herself. I sat on the puckered blue tuffet facing her, intoxicated by her mystery, inhaling the smoke, my eyes following the plumes as they vanished into the ceiling.

"And," said Mother, "she's a bad influence on Sandy." Mother, who hated the smell of cigarettes. Every time you looked at Aunt Rose, she was wearing something different, like a cutout doll. To thank me for sharing my room with her, she gave me a heart-shaped locket, which, years later, was in my purse on its way to the jeweler for repair when a man snatched the purse. I hung on until he pushed me and ran, and the police looked everywhere and couldn't find my lovely leather purse, much less the necklace. A rose was painted on the heart. My thrilling aunt. She died in an asylum.

# SIX WHITE HORSES

Aides herded us into the dayroom. A white-haired lady was playing on a piano, a piano that wasn't there before. Although we hated the status quo, change frightened us. The unknown person smiled as we filled the room thinking, *Now what are we in for?* Then my eyes met with hers and we froze, her face turning as white as her hair. She looked like Miss Edwards, my childhood piano teacher. Immediately I thought, *Mother won't like it that someone from the outside knows I'm here.*

First, Miss Edwards, if that's who she was, coaxed us to sing "Camptown Races." I'd sung that song on the Town Hall lawn with my Gates Mills day campers, ten, twelve years ago. It was unbearable to sing the same song here. Plus, as children, we sang a lot better than this bunch of loonies.

*Camptown races five-mile-long*
*Doo dah, doo da*
*All the do da day.*

When Mother came, I blurted out, "Miss Edwards was here."

"What?!"

"Miss Edwards, the piano teacher."

"Miss Edwards—here? Sandy, Miss Edwards studied with Arthur Rubinstein! She wouldn't be in this—"

"She made us sing."

"Is this true? What did she look like?"

I touched my hair. "White waves. Why did she come here? There was a lump in my throat. I couldn't sing."

"Dear heaven. I can't believe it. That revered teacher here. I'll find out her schedule. You can comb your hair. Will you do that, Sandy? Comb your hair if Miss Edwards comes again? I'll ask an aide to help you. What a shock for her…and what if she talks?"

*She'll be drivin' six white horses when she comes—Whoo whoo.*
*She'll be drivin' six white horses when she comes—*
*Oh, we'll all go out to meet her Oh we'll all go out to meet her*
*Oh, we'll all go out to meet her when she comes—*

I asked Mother in my please-don't-be-mad-at-me voice, "Is someone coming to meet us?"

"Yes, Sandy," her voice muffled and low, as though speaking from a long time ago.

"When, Mama, when will someone come?"

"When she comes."

# GOD'S COUNTENANCE

Sometimes I miss it—yes, I do—Mount Sinai's locked ward where we broke the commandments of sanity, worshipped the golden calf of clinical self-indulgence, each of us listening to our own burning bush and no one else's, our minds enslaved by the pharaoh of internalized oppression. That murmur you hear after Lights Out—we are praying at the edge of the Red Sea:

O Lord, don't swallow me—let me cross to the Promised Land. Because aren't you the same God when I was in my best dress, sitting between my parents in a pew with some other family's name etched on the brass plate, and we chanted with the rabbi, '*Let Your countenance smile down upon us*—' And I worried that You would smile on the family who wasn't there, who was there in name only. Not us who were really there. My parents' goodness wouldn't fit on a stupid little show-off brass richer-than-thou nameplate, wouldn't fit on the Torah, the ark, where during the Mourners' Kaddish, the bereaved slowly stood—as though struggling with gravity as well as mortality—the chanted Hebrew flowing over their bowed heads, and they squeezed the back of the oak pew in front of them as though wood—if not God—could bend. Isn't Your countenance still in effect, Lord? Your smiling countenance? Is it or isn't it? I have to know.

It was a point of honor for me that I always got out of the hospital in thirty days. Talk about delusions. At some point, I learned thirty days was not about good behavior. It was all about insurance. But now we know. It's a gene. Okay, has everyone got that straight? It's not our fault. Even the doctors—we're all innocent!

That's why I'd shuffle through the double doors, ashen on my mother's arm, her purse stuffed with Thorazine. "Ta ta," to the uniformed doorman with his hand-grenade of keys. My fellow inmates, watching from the dayroom, eyes blazing like disbelieved prophets from the Bible. The cruelest blow is when someone just as crazy as you walks out those doors.

If my parents could have afforded a long-term policy, I might still be in the psych ward playing triple solitaire, screaming my fool head off. Or sketching the catatonics. And don't forget occupational therapy—my mother could have had a kitchenful of potholders. When Aunt Ruth visited, Mother could say, "Sandy made these. Here, take some. Take more." Because Aunt Ruth was in on the secret. So, her kind heart could break like her sister's, every time she lifted a pot from the stove.

*To An Insane Degree*

# MY SONG FOR CRAZY WRITERS

*Rachmaninoff, Roethke, Coward & Keats*

*Baudelaire, Hopkins, both Shelleys*
*& Edna oh Edna St Vincent Millay*

# THE COMPREHENSIVE

Back at Columbia by spring, 1961. Artist friends helped me tape clean, white paper on the studio walls. My paintings would be comprehensible. The baskets, the seashells, cream pitchers, ashtrays; the fleshy pink and terra verte, violet and viridian. The bitten apple on a bit of lace. The black-and-white still life painted between sleeping pills. The paintings that made me live so I would finish them.

    I waited outside in the hall while the teachers read my thesis and looked at the still lifes flowing into each other like they were all one painting. Which they were. The previous year, one student failed his comprehensive exam. It wasn't a given. Our tiny class of seven. Finally, our teachers came out; Heliker smiling his Zen smile. And my parents drove from Ohio with a case of champagne and a vase of violets from our woods.

# GIMBEL'S

I first saw the red coat in Gimbel's window. The new trapezoid shape of 1961, bouclé, self-covered buttons. The mannikin—if it was a mannikin—was wearing Jackie's pillbox hat, her trademark pearl choker. I was looking for a job, high from finally graduating, high from the comprehensive—high. I couldn't afford to rent a gown to graduate in, but that coat was a must.

The First Lady said to me, "I am the president's wife, and I'm not going out of style. I'm redecorating the White House. How many people can say that? You are a passerby. Your coat is thin, colorless, last year's. Most of all, everyone admires me. That's what you want, isn't it—to be admired? Buy this coat. It's still summer. They'll deduct it from your wages. Come fall, you'll be me."

Everyone knew employees get a twenty percent discount. I found a *Daily Mirror* in the trash and rifled through to see who Gimbel's was hiring: inventory clerk for Jewel Distributors of America. Must be good at details, fine handwriting a plus. (They could have saved some money on the ad if they'd known fine handwriting *means* good at details.) I pinned up my long hair and—poof: I was Mother, who could do no wrong. In the interview, I mimicked her competence and charm.

"My name is Diamond," I said. "I was born for this job."

The office of the inventory clerk was up a narrow winding stair, ending in a cubby hole above Gimbel's main floor, a miniature rickety mezzanine out of Dickens. The bookkeeper, Josephine, was a red-headed hunchbacked dwarf. She climbed up a high stool, fingers flying over her hand-cranked Victor Comptometer. This was before the Speedee Add-A-Matic or the Micro-Tally. Stooped white-haired Albert, silent as an egg, held Piaget, Cartier, and Steinhausen watches to his jeweler's glass-magnified eye, listening to time. The space was so small, two people couldn't stand at once or else the chairs would hit each other. When you intended to rise, you murmured, "Getting up."

After the eighth installment, the coat was mine. I modeled it for Josephine and Albert, swirling so the skirt flared and collapsed back on itself like a matador's cape, touching all our frightened chairs. As soon as I fastened the self-covered buttons in their buttonholes, nothing could hurt me.

---

Every morning, the mailboy dumped packages of gems on my desk for me to record in a ledger and price with tiny white price tags tied around each one. One day, I unwrapped a luminous hand-knotted pearl necklace and thought, "Mother would like these." I propped my purse open on my lap and waited until Albert and Josephine weren't looking. Just as I was about to slide the pearls into the purse, Albert said, "Getting up." Pretending to compare again the price tag in my fine hand to the wholesaler's inventory sheet, I waited for the one I called The Watchman to sit down again, his back to me.

Daddy wrote to me that Mother wore the pearls often—they went with everything. "Fannie and Babe can't get over the perfect roundness of each pearl, how perfectly they match, the light from within," Daddy wrote, in his elegant ascenders and descenders. "Maybe Sandy can get us a necklace too," they said.

He told me when the string broke how everyone helped pick up the pearls. One had even made it as far as the deli counter. Mother put the necklace in a brown paper bag and dropped it off at the jeweler upstairs in the shopping center. He was busy with a customer and she had to get back to the restaurant, so she put a note in the bag, asking him to re-string them when he got a chance. She was at the cash register when, minutes later, the jeweler leaned over the counter of two-cent mints, chewing gum, and the sanitary toothpick dispenser.

"For God's sake, Mrs. D," he whispered, "do you know what those pearls are worth? Please tell me they're insured. Because they have to be insured before I work on them. I don't think you know what you've got here. I can't help wondering how much corned beef Mr. D's been selling to afford this high-class piece of goods. It's none of my business, but if he can afford pearls like this, why doesn't he hire a cashier and take you on a cruise?"

---

I wasn't seeing my friends every day like I used to at school. Everyone moved, had new lives, new friends elsewhere. I rented a loft in Yorkville without knowing the neighborhood. With the landlord's permission, I painted the dingy walls white. Came home to see my shabby furniture huddled on the sidewalk, the lock changed. I went to a phone booth to call for help. The directory was in shreds, hanging from its chain like a suicide. In the wooden tray under the phone, someone had carved a swastika.

"Get me out of here," I sobbed from the booth, its doors folding around me. Had I called home? It would be dinnertime. Dianne at the table, praying the phone wouldn't ring.

*Sandy Diamond*

# CHARLES THE GUN COLLECTOR

It was a time again of eyes shut with speckled shells. Home again, wanting to die, reading mindless novels, killing time. Despite knowing what Thoreau said:
*You can't kill time without injuring eternity.*

Time I would not be able to make up. There is no summer school for the crazed. And then without warning—Mr. Hyde! He threw me off the bed and chased me down the hall to Charles' room—my brother Charles, the gun collector!

"This is it!" Hyde said. "Arm yourself! This is your moment. Your time has come."

*I used to amuse my little brother with stories of my life in New York while he sat on his bed, polishing his rifle stocks, the soft rag rubbing his beauties to a velvet sheen. He rubbed in time to Fats Domino singing on the Victrola "Ain't That A Shame?" His wallpaper, chosen when he was much younger—cowboys twirling lassoes, straddling fences, yodeling. One cowboy was falling off his fence. I think I could have handled it if it were just that once, but of course, being wallpaper, the cowboy fell over and over again. He never learned. My little brother and I felt the same way about his guns. They were objects of beauty, not weapons. Sometimes Dad and my brothers and I shot the empty tin cans of dinner off tree stumps beyond the orchard. I could still pull a trigger then.*

I don't remember if the cowboys had guns. It makes sense that they did. I grabbed the prettiest pistol—an etched silver Arabesque.

"Ammunition!" goaded Hyde—and a round tin of bullets—shiny blue lettering 500 Superpoint *Luftgehr Spitzkugeln*. I didn't know if they would fit the gun and I didn't know German. I raced back to my room, sat on the edge of my bed trying to make the bullets go in, and they wouldn't. Weeping, cursing, I screamed at the gun, "God damn you!"

"Sandy, who are you talking to?" asked Mother on the other side of the door in her darling-put-down-the-machete voice.

When I saw the gun wouldn't work, I thought they would call the cops. The cops would shoot tear gas through the keyhole. I drenched a hanky with perfume to tie around my nose and mouth. It must have been Jungle Gardenia, Lily of the Valley being too innocent. Crouching in the back of my closet, faint from a scent meant for glamour and romance, I tore off the hanky, gasping for breath.

No, they wouldn't call the cops. I heard my father's voice on the phone with Dr. Weiss. Then I heard him say to Mother, "He says, *Call the cops*."

Mother said, "No, we'll handle this ourselves."

Mother wouldn't want the neighbors to see policemen climbing a ladder to my window. We weren't that kind of family. This was Gates Mills, Ohio, population three thousand, where everyone painted their shutters green.

She yelled, "Michael, get the clothesline!"

*What was Michael doing there? He doesn't live here anymore. I'm not opening this door.*

"Hey there, Sandy, let me see you," his voice wheedling me like we were playmates again. "Just crack the door, so I can see you're okay."

"Don't do it!" cried Hyde.

Michael the favorite cared about me! I slipped the lock half an inch—

Suddenly, the door filled with a blanket covering the gun, and my brother and father fell on me, pinning me to the floor.

"Judas!" I screamed.

They were tying me up with the rope. "That's the clothesline!" I screamed.

My father was testing the knots.

"Is that too tight, honey?"

Something wet fell on my wrist. I looked up. My father was crying.

"Don't cry on me!"

I was flying apart, and they tied me in one piece. *Daddy, I hung your socks twisted as licorice from that line.* That day, they drove me thirty miles downtown on the back-seat floor of the family car in the family rope, the family mad girl me! Snowing. Mother tucked my coat around the side of beef everyone was pretending was me, reeking of the meat of my madness. Out the window, the bright stars of my village—*save me*, the next village, the townships, oh America, are you paying attention? The blurred stars of the suburbs and the smeared stars of the city, winking like it's all one big joke—fuck you, stars. I'll get even. I'll get out of this.

Out of the car, oh gently, Daddy, snowing here too—sweet cold dark air. They're sorry. I can feel they know they're making a big mistake. I'm their daughter—doesn't that mean anything anymore? Stairs, going down. A basement. Nothing like my childhood basement where once I heard Mother playing Chopin. I stood armless as a sausage. Someone pried out Daddy's knots. That must be the director behind a huge desk, his crazy papers in my face, my parents' faces pleading with me to sign. Why do they want you to sign yourself in like it's a hotel or something? Hell is hell, whoever admits you. He who used to be my father had his pen out writing in the air as though all I had to do was think of it as charades.

I snatched the papers and tore them to pieces—paper clips, staples, punched holes' reinforcements—nothing could stop me. Ecstatic with lawlessness, I swung my boots up on the director's desk. He was infuriated, an imposter (shouldn't he be used to temper tantrums by now?) the kindly real director bound and gagged in the closet? This madman was an inmate, my parents too awed by authority to catch on. Two aides appeared from nowhere, locked my arms behind me, and carried me with my feet in the air down a dank hall, a hall I recognized from *The Birdman of Alcatraz*. A thick door clanked open to reveal a narrow cell with cinder-block walls, no window. Or was there a tiny window high up, with bars, like Burt Lancaster's? A metal table, leather straps dangling from it.

"What is this?" My voice hoarse. Already I was changing from Jekyll to Hyde. Or the other way around.

# INGLESIDE 1960

"This is Seclusion. You asked for it." They both laughed—what did that mean?

Without warning—a quicker mind would have gotten the drift—they lifted me up as though I weighed nothing at all. It was almost fun as they fastened me to the table at ankles and wrists—the leather crusty, the buckles sharp. Yanking off my boots, they slammed the door behind them and I couldn't put my hands over my ears. The last thing I heard was the scrape of a key in a lock made for criminals; not me, not an artist with a fellowship, not someone who makes sure her little sister and brother are out of the house before she goes berserk.

*I see them trudging down the drive, snow plowed high on either side. They're holding hands. They are sad. They don't know what's going on. I held off until they were safe—I could do that. I fucking saved them.*

This was the second time I'd been hospitalized. The first time, I thought, *I can't believe this is happening.* Everything about it was new. But the second time, I thought, *I can't believe this is happening again.* Often, I spoke to Dr. Weiss in my mind. I called him The Questioner.

THE QUESTIONER: "Excuse me. I have a question."

*Oh no, not The Questioner here with me in Seclusion.*

"The fact is—"

*Facts! Don't make me laugh.*

"—the second pair of children were five and six years younger than you. If you were twenty-two, they were in their teens. Ergo: no hooded snowsuits."

*I got the children out of there. That is to my credit.* "Send the kids away!" I yelled. I saw their puffy snowsuits—hers pink, his navy blue—trudging down the drive. Now they must go to the neighbors' because I don't know what I'll do next. Leave fast, fast! Little sister revolving on my vanity stool, touching the perfume atomizers, dreaming in my round mirror, just as I did once, before the wrong things happened. Don't look in that mirror. Don't be me.

"But I saw them! I held back the organdy curtain so I could see them go."

"Was that an earlier time? Had this happened before?"

"I'm asking for your own good. People are going to want to know what actually happened and what you're making up."

"It *all* happened, especially the parts I made up. Imagination's in the mind, the mind's in the body and the body's real—I think that's a fact."

I never imagined killing my parents. It wasn't like that. The guns and knives, the broken bottle in the jagged bulging room at 113th Street—my roommate sweet-talking me, *Give me the bottle give me the bottle now, please!* The weapons were to ward off the madness. I wonder how many people are in prison for what I did, for self-defense?

*In the fifties, if you were male, you could be a rebel, but if you were female, your families had you locked up.*
—Gregory Corso

Columbia was waiting for me to finish my paintings. I thought I would die without ever painting again. Die without finding love. Without making my parents proud.

*She almost made it,* they'd say. *She might have made it. We'll never know. Feet on the director's desk—bad idea. Tearing up the commitment papers—a big mistake. This isn't Sandy. Our Sandy could have been someone.*

My painting master sent me a photograph of himself, dated January 1960. He's looking at something out of the picture. He sent a slender book, *Zen and the Art of Archery*. Mr. Heliker, I'll read it as soon as my eyes get in focus. Don't let anyone throw out my paintings. I'm coming back. I'll finish them. I will.

*…crazy is not a person, it is a place you go…*
—Emma Richler, *Sister Crazy*

Silence. The smell of ashes. The metallic taste of manic episodes. It's so cold, loathsome February. It's always February in mental institutions, four weeks of dreaming of kitchen knives, taxidermy, the open oven door, month of no leaves. Show me how to go back to how it used to be—crayoned valentines, scholastic keys, violets in a pale green vase. Is that lost forever? But how past is it if I'm her and not her at the same time, like someone in a movie newly dead, the mortal body on the street, the translucent spirit not knowing where to go, how to intervene? Tied to its former self, its lifelong burden and rare ecstasy, its hunger and satiety. Its despair. Its great loneliness. Its incoherence and the laughter that won't stop, even after everyone's left the room or wasn't there in the first place, visiting hour over, medicine cart coming—Mommy, Daddy, I'll be good. I'll be good.

*Don't think about it,* Daddy used to say. *Don't think about it, don't talk about it. Keep it to yourself. I had lit a box of Kleenex on fire and dropped it down the stairwell on my family eating dinner. The motion blew the flame out by the second stair. What a failure as a maniac I turned out to be. And a failure at sanity. What's left?*

Next day—if that's what it was—I heard the sound of a key scratching in its hole—a door creaked open. A big dark man unbuckled the straps, peeled me off the table like a paper doll. Holding my arm, he flew me after him into the hall, stopping at a small, flimsy curtain, a stench like my own magnified. He pushed me through the cloth.

"I'll be right here, girl, so don't try anything."

I wanted to say, "My daddy owns the Tasty Shop—he'll get you for this." But I was too scared to speak. I was a girl with vomit in her hair, holding her breath, staring at a toilet black with filth. My body ached with its imperfect holding-back. The curtain was a foot too short for privacy. What is better—to get a terrible disease or burst? That was the kind of choice available to me. Mother never trusted public toilets. She taught me to straddle when away from home. But this toilet—so foul, the mad, grief-stricken excrement could pull me into its fetid maw. I would never tell Mother about this if I lived. The aide stood one foot from the other side of the curtain. When the stream burst from me, he laughed like he was in an opera.

Back in the cell, but not on the table. Free! Everything's relative. Now I could see the peephole in the door. I knew when someone was watching me by the blocking of the light. I acted for that audience. Calm but not abject. Self-contained, not something they owned. I stood by the table to show it was too high for me to get back up on by myself. Even if I wanted to. Which of course, I didn't. Why would I? Why would anyone? They can't hold that against me. Lying on the table—now *that* would be crazy. I could stand by the table, fold my arms on it, and lay my head in my arms. How would that be? Neither on the table nor abandoning it. As if to say, I'm acknowledging your table but am not completely under its sway.

Smile. Smile. But how much? Not vacant. It must be an inhabited smile. It must say: I am like you. Please don't hit me. Let me out. We could be two people meeting at a party or a dance—yes, like at the junior prom, when a blister from my new shoes burst and spilled blood on the gym floor from the first and last two-inch heels I'll ever have, and everyone pointed and stared and laughed like they did when I couldn't jump onto the padded horse. Once I was happy, admired, laughing. I had a doll who loved me.

Examine the walls! I may never get a chance like this again. Maybe there was a chink, like at the Wailing Wall where God reads the messages, so they say—and there was a note in the chink! That would mean—aha!—someone was here before me and someone—oh God—will come after.

What's in my pocket? This lump. A book of matches! The cover says, *Draw Me*. I'm sick and tired of everyone telling me what to do. The profile of a girl with a turned-up nose and fluffy hair. She looked like the girls in junior high who made fun of me. I used to draw that face. I didn't know any better. I wanted to be a Famous Artist, not that I mailed in my drawing for a free evaluation. That's how much confidence I had. When was it that I noticed Jews don't have turned-up noses? Probably because God didn't give us anything to be stuck up about. If only I could have turned up my nose at madness. There seems to be a disproportionate number of Jews in mental hospitals and a disproportionate amount of Jewish psychiatrists. What does that tell you? I don't know, maybe nothing. But I know this: Jews don't buy houses with cathedral ceilings. My people like our ceilings low so nothing can fall on us from a great height.

I slid my hand into the far pocket, found a blue coupon that said, "Keep This Coupon, Admit One." Well, I'm already admitted, baby. A ticket to enter a movie or circus. To be part of something. The note in the chink said, "Help me. I'm sorry for what I did." Not knowing what she did. It could have been anyone. Other ankles, other wrists were fastened here. The next inmate to come—with nothing to wipe her tears with—what can I give her? This coupon I don't dare take from my pocket, assuming it's there. I know—on the back I'll write in my mind—my mind!—"You'll get out."

Now I saw the source of light, however feeble. I felt like a nightlight in the half-light of dusk, and I don't know if I should go on or not. A square window, tiny, with bars, high up, the walls thick as the sandcastle walls Michael and I built in Miami Beach long ago as the ocean crept up on us to wash our castle away. Will I never stop harping on the past? I hear the sacred flow of American traffic. All the people driving downtown to try on dresses. I used to be one of them. Someone else lay here, listening to my Renault Dauphine, watching a smudge on the concrete wall. So, you who are now there could one day be here. Ha!

I failed geometry. Thanks to you, Euclid, I had no summer my junior year of high school. How do you like it that all these loonies are locked up on the street of your name? You who tried to show us how to be rational, you who created order.

You know what order means to me? Orders at the Tasty Shop, shouted to Abie, the counterman at his meat slicer.

"*Corned beef on rye, hold the fat!*"

*Slicing off the thin white ribbon of fat by hand slowed Abie down.*

"*Why is the fat there anyway?" I asked him.*

"*God put the fat there! You think you know better than God?*"

*The bluish numbers blurring on his arm slicing corned beef, pastrami and tongue, his family kaput, and most of his teeth.*

"*Roll your sleeve down," I silently begged, as if telepathy might really work just this once.*

# THE ROAD TO NANTES

I'm ten years old at the Cleveland Museum of Art. Every Saturday after Art for Gifted Children, I went to see *The Road to Nantes*. Pierre Bonnard. He tilts the horizon so you are flung onto the road, catapulted into the distance. The brushwork suggests a presence in the sky. At the same time that I'm in the museum, I'm on this road in France. There's a fork in the road. You can turn off on a side street or continue up the hill. What to do? If life has it in for you, age is no protection. There was always a gray uniformed guard behind me. Did he think a child would steal the painting? He with his gold buttons. The painting was small, but the frame was heavy—carved and ornate. It wasn't going to fit under my coat—even the baggy raincoat. Even if I could have reached that high to lift it off its hanger. But what if it were in my bedroom? I saw myself waking up to that road every day.

One day, on the floor under *The Road to Nantes*, there was a vase with a single white lily.

"What's the meaning of this?" I asked the guard.

"The artist died this week."

Pierre Bonnard died? So, he was alive! I didn't think of any of those artists in the museum as being alive. Bonnard had been living in the same world as me, at the same time. I could have written to him and asked how he mixed those dusky blues. And which way he would have taken on the road. Now it was too late. I was here, going nowhere. Bonnard signed his name like a child in printed letters following the angle of the road.

Did Bonnard plan ahead? Did he plan for the road to fork? Maybe he meant it doesn't matter which way you go. If you don't get to Nantes this way, then go *this* way. Eventually, you'll get to Nantes. We have to believe this.

In *The Artist in His Studio*, there is a photograph of Bonnard. A frail-looking man in a big scarf, huddled by a small radiator. He didn't use a palette or an easel. He nailed his canvas to the wallpaper—no preconceived size. Mixed his colors on a dinner plate. Tacked up on the wall were crumpled squares of tinfoil from candy wrappers. Why did he do this? I did it too, to find out. When the sunlight hit the foil, the squares blazed and shot out rays so fierce, my eyes hurt. He was trapping light; trapping light and letting it go.

*Sandy Diamond*

# BRAIDS UNRAVELED

*Past leaves too pretty to walk on, crickets, lizards and frogs, spiders, beetles, and bugs, scurrying on the cat-soft moss. There were tame rocks that let you stand on their glossy backs and wild rocks that bucked you right off. In the shady damp, Michael's hair curled tight as fiddlehead ferns; my braids unraveled, rubber bands lost to ants bearing off the alien elastic loops. Everything was something else and we, most of all: changelings. We were headed for No-Touch Hill.*

My mother, who braided my hair every morning and let the school bus and all the cars behind it wait on Wilson Mills Road until my hair was up to her standard. My father, who lifted me—suede chaps, fringed vest, and red cowboy hat with adjustable string—to the saddle of a horse at Sleepy Hollow Ranch on County Line Road, fit my boots in the stirrups and put the reins in my hands. Samuel and Elizabeth, who wanted their children to grow up in the storybook village of Gates Mills, with its hillsides of flowering dogwood each spring. Where the Cleveland Indians' legendary pitcher Bob Feller lived. Michael and I kept turning the Wheaties box so the baseball star looked at us during his wind-up.

The same parents who listened on the other side of the locked bathroom door:

"Are you alright, dear? Please come out now."

This was not the kind of family that forced locked doors. Mother tried the knob soundlessly while I held a thin blue Gillette to the blue of my wrist, whispering, "Let me go, let me go," hating them for the love that was stronger than suicide.

*The arbitrary naps of kindergarten. We folded our arms on the table and lay our heads on our arms. Teacher said she would walk behind us and lift each child's finger to see if we were really asleep. I thought if I was sleeping,*

*I'd have no will, so I left my finger in the air where she had put it. Maybe by first grade, I'd understand how the world worked. My snowsuit had a soft brown furry collar the size of two hamsters. To feel that furriness, my best friend, Tomma, buttoned and unbuttoned my coat every time we went indoors and out.*

At home I rotated my silverware, giving each one a chance to get out of the drawer. Not always bearing the weight of the others on top of it. See, God, I cared for your smallest creatures. Let me go. Once, I was your darling. I climbed trees to be closer to you, to see what you were up to in your high heaven. I've seen the sun and the moon in the sky at the same time! And I'm not the only one.

Others speak for me. I used to cry when Pinocchio said, "I'm a real boy at last!" Maybe Stan will hold me on his lap again, one last time. Dr. Weiss said we've tried everything but ECT. The fight went out of me. The first time they started talking shock, I was high. I told my parents if they signed the papers, I'd kill them. That was the end of that. What elation, power, fear. Now I was depression's dead meat and I didn't care how they cooked me. I did not consent. I acquiesced. I was in Ingleside, no Dr. Weiss.

Shock drops down fast as a guillotine, separating the head from the body. It cleans the brain like an Electrolux, empties it by suction—memory, a vacuum. How precious turning over, curling up became. Even now. Gel smeared on your temples like lard—the bit in your mouth, separating the tongue from the teeth. This is what protection has come down to. Well, silly, they don't want to injure the tongue, which must squeal on and on to the doctors, the residents, the interns, aides, the fucking concrete walls.

I remember the paper shoes. I remember the bit in the mouth. I can still see the other patients shuffling back from the machine, after their little nap, of course, in their paper shoes. When it was my turn to feel the electricity surge and shudder through my body, that's how I must have looked to the others: Empty-eyed. Not giving a damn.

The mothers murmured the names of their children—*Ronnie, Donna, Marie*—trying to remember.

*Once, afterward, when I was back in the world again, I met a man at a party. He was instantly familiar with me. I'd never seen him before. He described the dresser where I laid the pins from my hair. He described my body in the mirror. I'd never seen him before in my life.*

Although no one would admit it at the time, the current opinion is that brain cells don't grow back. Even when you leave the hospital. Even when you have something really important to say. Or ever. I always thought I should be smarter than I am.

I knew this much: To be depressed is to say, *It's not worth it*. To be manic is to say, *It is worth it*. An argument no one can win. Thorazine kept me within human range for twelve years. I couldn't remember anything. That was the price of sanity for all those years of trying not to be Mr. Hyde.

# NO-TOUCH HILL

*You had to get a running start at the foot of No-Touch Hill, bending forward for momentum. Skittering stones try to trip you up. If you had to save yourself from falling, and your hand touched a pebble or a root, the watcher at the bottom cried, "Touched! You touched!" You skidded back down to the foot of the hill, which stretched above you taller than ever, and try again.*

Recovering from shock in the childhood playroom my father had made for Michael and me, Bob Dylan's first album was released, *The Dumb Waiter* opened on Broadway, and *One Flew Over the Cuckoo's Nest* was published. Stuff was happening on the moon, the world going on without me. Mother brought me a letter from Howie, his jerky I'm-kicking-heroin handwriting, the lines of script shattered by incomprehensible spaces. He wrote he saw Stan's mother at Stan's funeral. Her hair had turned white overnight. So now we know that really happens. The story came to me in jagged pieces. Stan had been offered to head the Philosophy Department at a university in Brazil. All his friends were excited for him; the prestige, the chance to travel. He wanted to stay in New York and write plays. He couldn't decide, Howard wrote. He was twenty-four.

I imagined him—so young. That's how we'll always imagine him. In the subway, knowing it was the last subway ride of his life. How does that feel? He got off at Canarsie Street. Before the cheap hotel, he found a pawnshop. Some fucking bastard sold my Stan a shotgun. Ammunition. He was always there for me. I wasn't there. Stan, who would have chopped down my door to save me, who held me on his lap and fed me like a baby, built crates for my paintings—how many times? I don't even know a measurable fact like that.

Howard wrote: Stan and I knew each other since we were fourteen. He was the only one who visited me when I was in the nuthouse. But I did not reciprocate his love when he needed it most, when he was cracking up. He shot his head off with a shotgun à la Hemingway, in a rundown Brooklyn hotel.

He had tried twice before!!! I was brusque or nostalgic when he tried to tell me what he was feeling. I killed Stan like I killed Elise Cowan, who jumped in February from her parents' seventh-floor window. Both kids died for the same reason. They had chosen paths in life abhorrent to their beatific ideals.

I had met Elise Cowan the summer of 1960—golden girl, her poetry already recognized—when she visited me in Gates Mills along with Keith, Eli, and Howie on their way to California. I see her running down the path to the lake—her light hair flying—to Keith, her lover then. They had all graduated in the spring. Delayed-by-madness, I had a year to go.

Keith and I stood on the sand at the edge of the lake, drawing spirals with our toes. Our friends diving from the raft made the water ripple, beckon, caress our feet.

"Take me with you," I said.

Keith said, "Go back to New York and get your degree. You must work out your servitude."

*The happiest part of your letter,* Howie wrote, was *"the paint will never dry up for me."* He wrote:

*I will not mourn for dead*
*if I mourn I go mad*
*if I go mad I can't function*
*same with you. how is sex life? are you thin or chubby?*
*don't pull any suicide bit of flipping out before calling me. [phone number]*
*love, howard*

The hysterical gout returned. A breeze from the door opening made me scream. Mother fed me thin soup through a pleated straw. I blame Beckett, his despair—Stan's blue ink underlines in *Molloy*—*the unraveling of ourselves*. I knew blaming Beckett was stupid—he lived to write more books, more plays. That's the part Stan didn't see.

# STILL LIFE FOR STAN

Seashell, ashtray, box of Chinese tea. The blue-and-white flowered ashtray floats on its shadow an inch from the left edge of the canvas. On the right edge, an egg-shaped speckled seashell, one brushstroke veering into space. Orange sun or moon on the tea box glows. The four shapes form a loose cross, pull away from each other, impasto from years of overpainting. Above it, a shadow cast by something we can't see.

At some point, Dianne bought the painting. When I missed it, she loaned it back to me. I couldn't bear that dark shadow. It was ugly. I wanted Stan's painting to be beautiful. I unfastened the canvas from its stretchers and cut off the top third, re-stretched. The memory of the shadow haunted me. Dianne didn't want the cut-down version back. She said I could keep it.

I saved Howard's letter. Here's the part I forgot: Stan had tried to take his life twice before. All my raving, *if only I was there*—I was there and still didn't know. The day he marked those passages in *Molloy*, he was already wounded, already defecting. Would a real bed have made a difference or if I had been more experienced in love? Such niceties meant nothing to me when *I* wanted to die. I was experienced in going mad—that's why he came to me. And I couldn't see it.

# WATERFALL

Now we could hear the waterfall trickling from God's fist. Like how we used to make trees from sand and water on our beach. All the rain in Cuyahoga County gathered and plunged through the woods to the shale ledges and poured its curtains of water faster than horses, faster than fairies.

On top of the hill we lay in lush ferns, panting like ponies, then still as moss. The tumbling water drenched the air. We breathed it in, filmy, diaphanous, felt the mist on our cheeks, our child bodies sinking into the perishable earth. The waterfall lets down her watery hair, streams between banks to the Chagrin River.

Teach me, Waterfall.

She says, "When you can't go any farther, become something else."

*The first summer I was here there were no flowers so I started picking up bones.*

*—Georgia O'Keeffe, At Abiquiu*

# ROUTE 66

An episode of *Route 66* was filmed two miles from my home where a new freeway was being built—primordial forms, craggy rebar, cantilevered concrete suspended as though to say anything can happen. Life—the next direction you take—is being formed before your eyes. You could get on the freeway here where it begins at Mayfield Village and keep driving until a sign says "Route 66." I had a crush on Buz, the character based on Jack Kerouac. The actor, George Maharis, resembled my past idol at the height of the series' fame.

The on-site caterer was the Tasty Shop. My job was to cook the best steak money could buy on a little hibachi bought for this purpose. Cast iron hibachis were a new invention in the early sixties. Everyone knew from movie magazines George Maharis was recovering from hepatitis and needed rare steak.

A few teenage daughters of the well-connected were allowed on the set. Except for the piece of meat, I had no status. On one show Buz had said "Who wants status? You've got status. You've got strings. You've got strings, you're a puppet."

That's how he talked. Very Kerouac. These girls were too young to have heard of Sal Paradise, too giggly for the actual live Kerouac to kiss their braid if they had had one, which they didn't. They waved their flowered autograph books at him.

"Buz! Buz!" they cried. A girl in a sleeveless blouse on this cold day stuck out her hussy arm and said, "Make it to Gwennie!" He held her arm steady and scrawled his name all the way up. Eventually, she'd have to wash that dumb-ass arm and she'd be nobody again. Whereas my healing meat would enter his body. The freeway was new; the hibachi was new. It had to mean I was going somewhere I'd never been before.

That was the day I learned you can't cook a rare steak and daydream at the same time. I rehearsed in my mind: "Here's your steak, Mr. Maharis. I'm sorry it's a bit overdone, but just on one side—see, my darling. If you don't like it, please don't tell my parents—that's my father watching over there. He bid on this job because he knows I love you. I hunger for adventure and romance just like you."

Mr. Maharis is cutting the steak now, his suntanned hands like California.

"Delicious," he said to Father. Buzz licked his TV lips because of me, dear god!

"Good job," he said.

## 1956. AIN'T WE ALL?

Someone fixed me up with Mac, a Korean War vet. He hailed from Painesville, Ohio, a small town south of Cleveland. We sat in the sun in my backyard, me turning twenty in a candy-striped sundress. Having dated only schoolboys and seen no action, I didn't know how to make conversation with a grown-up soldier. He was quiet and grave as a commemorative coin.

Mac told me a story from just before the war: he was an actor and had grown a beard for a role in Shakespeare, a year or two before beards were in vogue. He'd taken the bus to the Cleveland Greyhound Terminal, where a young man with a goatee rushed through the crowd, pumped his hand, and said,

"Where you from, man?"

"Painesville," Mac said.

And the beatnik said, "Ain't we all, man, ain't we all."

Mac coaxed a Lucky from its target pack, lit up. I hadn't started smoking yet. We didn't talk, the smoke another presence among us. I couldn't take my eyes off his mouth where his lips met around the Lucky, as though it was me he was inhaling. Desire wrenched me like pain, the coin of him rising. When the Lucky was down to a pinch, he shredded the tobacco remains in the mown grass and ate the paper.

"Field stripping," he said. "That's what you do in war. So the enemy can't find you."

I loved how he explained things without lecturing or making it my fault. So now the enemy was here in Gates Mills—amid the swings and monkey bars, the sandbox and wading pool my father had created. Mother brought out lemonade, then left, discrete as ever. Was she thinking it would be nice to have a good-looking son-in-law? Maybe he could be the night manager we were always on the lookout for.

Mac, I want to be ten years older—then would I know how to make love stronger than war? In a few years, my craziness would be in effect. Perhaps then the madness of war would make more sense to me. Mac was here in my backyard, the safest place on earth. His war stayed inside him like the Tasty Shop refugees with Auschwitz in their backs. Ain't we wounded, ain't we lonely, ain't we all, man, ain't we all.

# THE ALCAZAR

By Labor Day 1963, I was passing for normal. New friends, who didn't know my history—"You know who would be perfect for Sandy?"—fixed me up with Marv: intelligent, funny, good-looking, and sexy. M is the most forgiving letter—two peaks. Two chances to ascend, baby. No other letter has that. And he always lived up to his name.

I had been living with my parents, but as soon as I met Marv, I ran out and got a basement apartment on Surrey Road in Cleveland Heights, across the street from the historic Alcazar Hotel. The living room had a surreal view of footwear and dogs and cats strolling by on four legs. Lovely old bricks lightly whitewashed, suggesting a theater set.

For the first time in my life, I was in love on New Year's Eve, dancing with Marv at the Alcazar. We drifted out to the courtyard to smoke—though we didn't have to go out in 1963—nipped by December's smiling teeth. His silver lighter in the shape of the Manhattan skyline, my gold-tipped pastel Sherman. After our subterranean passion, he'd reach for that skyline, a gleam on the nightstand. The smoke lay above us like ourselves immaterial. Marv was always there for me, as smoking was there, to give me substance. Of course we smoked—everyone smoked. Why wouldn't you want to look like a free thinker in a foreign film, someone who knew what to do with her mouth?

At the countdown to midnight, the ceiling dissolved in a drift of silver balloons, membranes of the old year's air. Then confetti—everyone suddenly unrecognizable, lashes and cheeks veiled. Dancing, we clung, then spun away, confetti stuck to us like snow-dome snow, like pointillism.

Later in bed, a blue paper dot rested in the hollow of his hip.

"Your hip right there," I said, "is my favorite part of men's bodies."

He seemed a little disappointed, shivered when I took the dot with my tongue from the spot where—wrestling—the angel touched Jacob. That was the night, oh holy, we named the children we would have.

In a genuine imitation leatherette booth at the Tasty Shop, January 11, 1964, Marv and I read "The Report on Smoking and Health" in the *Cleveland Plain Dealer*. Fearful of Wall Street's reaction, the government broke the news on a Saturday. The waitresses wheezed by, swinging in and out the kitchen's double doors. They always left their cigarettes burning in an ashtray on a highchair in the back, and stole drags between courses.

Marv said, "Glamour and sophistication died with the real president. He would have figured out a way to protect the people, without scare tactics like this."

The possibility—no, certainty—of a life with Marv burst like cherry trees in fast-motion photography. I bought vintage blue-and-white china, Paul Revere silverware—no bridal registry for manics.

---

Suddenly Marv's father died. Sitting shiva at his mother's apartment, I instantly bonded with her. She pulled out photo albums of baby Marv, little cowboy Marv, etc., the actual Marv groaning, "Don't show her that!"

Her friends and family crowding around to see. I kept myself from telling her, "We've named the children! Your family will live on."

I felt everyone's heart lifting because of me. Felt them thinking, "At last, a nice Jewish girl for Marv."

Everything was going my way. I made sure not to eat too many canapes nor take the biggest ones. And then I saw that a framed painting on the wall was tilted. I got up from the sofa and straightened it. A seascape, too realistic for my taste, but it would be wrong to leave it askew. Then I realized the picture next to it was crooked as well. I nudged the left bottom corner of the frame up half an inch.

And looked back at the roomful of mourners who were all looking at me. I thought they would be smiling or at least nodding approval, but I couldn't tell what their expressions meant. I looked at Marv—he was holding up one hand and shaking his head. I thought that meant, "Go on." I continued evening up the next picture and suddenly Marv was standing with his arm too tight around me.

*To An Insane Degree*

He said, "It's time to go." He didn't even let me say goodbye to his mother. Outside on the wrought iron landing where no one could hear, he was crying.

He said, "I can't do this. You're crazy. You're too crazy for me. It's over."

---

Did I tell you about the potted palm shivering in the garden at the Alcazar?

A frond licked my bare shoulder. Laughable—a palm tree in Cleveland—but it meant anything was possible, don't you think? You have to understand about the Alcazar: Cole Porter had a suite there in the thirties. He wrote *Night and Day* there. That's a fact. He would have strolled in the courtyard, just like Marv and me, smoking with his long ivory cigarette holder.

*Night and day, you are the one.*

I've forgotten what we named the children.

The lost years of my twenties, the gaps every boyfriend fell into, out of. Which one was The One Who Could Have Been Forever? I forgot my bargain with God. Since God was the only one who knew about the bargain, it could only have been God who made me mad.

Sandy Diamond

# A SCREAMY TIME OF YEAR

I got a job at Fein Art Supply in Shaker Heights, a wealthy suburb of Cleveland. Warm and fun-loving, the owners became like second parents to me. Or maybe I make everyone that way: *Take care of me.* Under a façade of independence. *I am perfectly normal*, I kept telling myself.

I was one college graduate whose studies paid off. I stretched canvases, demonstrated how to mix colors. I talked my customers out of cheap, floppy brushes into pricey Kominsky sable—"The finest hairs from the animal's tail, caught by the brush maker as they run over the snowy steppes of Siberia. That chase is in this brush's spring—responsive to your every stroke."

Stage makeup was a sideline at the store—Max Factor's mustaches and eyebrows, werewolf crepe hair, spirit gum, tins of rouge. In October, we got a delivery of high-quality latex masks: over-the-head images of President Kennedy, the First Lady with optional pillbox hat and pearl choker, Khrushchev, the Beatles, astronauts, and Marilyn Monroe. Marilyn dead a year ago, year alive again, her electric, pouty lips parted to sing, "Happy Birthday, Mr. President." The arrow-through-the-head joke, capsules of blood. I never got tired of the gun joke: when you pulled the trigger, a flag came out that said, "*BANG!*"

The biggest hits were the Fab Four. You knew when school was out—suddenly the store was full of teenage girls who wanted to be Paul. If they didn't get one of his masks, they'd throw their arms around whoever *was* Paul and say, "I love you! Marry me!" It was a screamy time of year. You could be whoever you wanted.

Once, all four Beatles were singing and dancing *I Want to Hold Your Hand*. My bosses were trying on the President and First Lady masks. I went into a dream: The Beatles are shaking hands with the President.

Mrs. Fein is thanking Mrs. Kennedy for charming the French Minister of Culture into loaning the Mona Lisa to the United States earlier that year. I wore the Marilyn Monroe mask, a blond wig, the flouncy curls I always wanted. What if my paintings were good enough someday, famous enough for me to be a mask? Marilyn was thirty-six. I was twenty-five—eleven years to go. No, I'm a nobody. If I were a Halloween mask displayed on a Styrofoam head, people would say,

"Who is that supposed to be?"

# MONA LISA

The Mona Lisa got so many love letters, she was the only work of art in the Louvre to have her own mailbox. Once, a brokenhearted suitor shot himself in front of her. When the Mona Lisa was stolen from the Louvre in 1911, the iron pegs on which the portrait had hung were kept on display behind the velvet rope. People thronged to stare at the wall where she had been. They left flowers. Kafka came from Prague to gaze at the empty space with his haunted eyes. The French border was barricaded, departing ships and planes searched. The far-right newspapers blamed the Jews. The young Picasso and wild Apollinaire—who had just invented the term *Surrealism*—had signed a manifesto, exhorting the burning of the Louvre—were suspects interrogated by the police. Chorus lines made up with the face of Mona Lisa danced topless in the cabarets of Paris. The whole affair was Kafkaesque.

It turned out that an Italian, Vincenzo Peruggia, had spirited off the painting because he thought Napoleon had stolen it from Italy for the French. The thief, hailed in Italy as a patriot, didn't serve time for his crime. He died soon afterward from lead poisoning. The Mona Lisa enjoyed a triumphant tour of Italy before returning to France. I'd never thought about why this most famous painting by an Italian was in the Louvre instead of the Uffizi.

# PAINT BY NUMBER

Fein Art Supply was my favorite job ever. Salesmen gave me samples of their new products, asking which varnish or fixative I liked best. Customers took my advice. What power. The one thing I despised was Paint by Numbers and their motto: *Every man a Rembrandt.*

"*Paint by Numbers,*" I informed my bosses, "are to real painting how mannikins are to real people."

"This fad will be the death of art!" Unaware at the time that da Vinci invented this scheme of mixing little pools of color to teach his students composition. "How can you call yourself a fine art supply store? What would van Gogh say to little numbers all over his sacred sunflowers? Or Monet, who is all about no borders—reduced to sections with pre-assigned hues—the exact *opposite* of Impressionism?"

"His *Water Lilies* are one of our top sellers," Mrs. Fein said. She was leafing through the *Paint by Numbers Index.* "You seem to be a bit of a snob, my dear."

Mr. Fein said, "You seem to have forgotten we are in business to make money."

"Speaking of making money, I want a raise."

"A raise? Already you want a raise? You haven't even been here a year."

"Asking for a raise is a sacred American tradition."

"And saying, 'Ask me in another six months' is another American tradition."

"Do you think Gertrude Stein waited six months before asking for a raise?"

"Gertrude Stein?" Mrs. Fein said. "Gertrude Stein never worked a day in her life!"

"Who is she?" Mr. Fein said to his wife. "Do we know her? Who names a girl *Gertrude* anymore?"

By now I realized my timing was wrong. "Well, if she had *wanted* a job, she wouldn't have come *here*."

"Good!" Mr. Fein said. "Because I wouldn't hire her."

Mrs. Fein turned to me. "Someone with no work experience, why should we hire? We already got you. Isn't she the one who said, 'The difference, to be a difference, must *make* a difference?'"

Mr. Fein replied, "What difference does it make? I don't want her."

Mrs. Fein slapped down her index. "Anyway, she's not that famous. There's no Paint-by-Number of her."

## WHERE WERE YOU?

I was inventorying the archival thirty-two by forty Crescent matboards, sliding each color out a few inches to see what colors were low. My hand was on Bar Harbor Gray—my favorite—when the bell over the door rang and a man's voice cried, "They got him! They shot Kennedy!" I looked up in time to see him run to the next door. The Feins were running out from the back room crying, "*No!*"

Three weeks later—in time for Christmas sales—a shipment of Paint by Numbers, the salesman proud of the new seascapes and bouquets. Lifting each kit into Mr. Fein's hands, a little assembly line of non-art.

Suddenly, Mr. Fein snapped, "No! Take this one back," starting to hand a box back to the salesman, who threw up his hands.

"Mr. Fein, you know our arrangement—the full shipment must be accepted."

"Not this one. It's unacceptable." He was holding it up too high for Mrs. Fein and me to see.

"What is it, Louie?" Mrs. Fein said, "Let me see."

He held the box higher. "I won't have it in my store. Get it out of here!"

What could make Mr. I'm-in-business-to-make-money reject merchandise?

"It'll be a big hit with your clientele, my friends. It's setting Paint by Number records."

Mrs. Fein grabbed the box, tilting it. I saw numbers on the president's face, on his hair, his teeth, his boyish smile.

*Sandy Diamond*

# BEVERIX

It was my musician friend Michael Dreyfuss of the flaming violin who fixed me up with Bob Everix, known as Beverix. Michael told me about my blind date's name, so even before I saw him, I loved the contraction—something drawn together, something left out. We met at a birthday party. I was standing near the cake when I saw a man with Mohawk cheekbones. Craggy, graceful, self-contained. In the time it took Michael to introduce us, a girl walked between us. Without breaking her stride, she ran her finger along the bottom of the cake, licked the frosting off her finger, and kept walking. It was May, dear Lord; I should have gathered a sugar rosette while I could. I fell for Beverix beyond all reason.

He taught English and Philosophy at Lake Erie College for Women. I bet all his students had a crush on him. We couldn't stop talking to each other, as though we knew there was so little time. I guess he knew, but I didn't. That first night we lay in my bed telling each other everything we'd seen and done. Then I heard a noise. "What's that?"

"Sounds like a bird," he said. The bird was telling me people have lives like this, in love, not alone. Even me.

We'd talked all night. That's how it was every night, lying in the bed, facing the whitewashed brick wall I'd faced with Marv. I'm getting another chance, I thought. This year I already had a depression so if I could keep from getting high, maybe Beverix was the one who'd last. I loved how his names contained the word ever. As in *forever*.

Finally one night I touched him. He whispered, "Not yet. Let's be how we are."

Dreyfuss wouldn't have fixed us up if Beverix were gay, right? It was me; I was too eager. I had to learn the patience of his name that had something left out, the contract that we sleep together, but not make love.

To An Insane Degree

# MEMORIAL DAY

It was Memorial Day weekend. No school—I thought that meant Beverix and I would be together. It meant he had to grade finals. I looked in the garage for a ladder, but couldn't find one. With the copy of *Zen and The Art of Archery* Mr. Heliker had given me, I climbed up to the roof of my apartment building's garage. There was a short brick wall on which I balanced an upside-down empty trash can. I had just read the part in the book where the youth climbs to the mountain cave to ask the master swordsman to teach him the art of self-defense. Like all those tales of Zen enlightenment, the youth is assigned lowly tasks—sweeping the cave, cleaning the huge cooking pot. After a year of this, the lad asks the master when can he learn the secrets of the warrior. From then on the master gives the boy no peace, creeping up behind him as he chops kindling and hitting him with a big stick. Another year passes, the youth trying to guard against the surprise attacks. One day, polishing the giant lid of the cooking pot, he sees in the shiny metal the reflection of his teacher sneaking up on him with his raised sword. The youth whirls, the lid deflects the blow.

*"Go back to the world,"* the master says. *"I've taught you all I know."*

I'd just bought a white piqué bathing suit with red laces at the thighs and breast. I could make them as tight or loose as I wanted. I found it at William Kitt's on Shaker Square—that's how ritzy it was. Those were the days before we knew better than to bathe in the sun. I had failed so much, but I tanned well. I was tan as toast. Looking up at the sky, I heard a small plane humming high above white shreds of clouds. Would the pilot look down and see me, still as a painting of a sunbathing girl? Thirsty, I thought I'd climb down for water. *Easy,* I told myself. *Be sure your foot is on the center of the trash can.*

Something moved, tipped, slid; I was falling. Ten feet apparently isn't enough for your whole life to flash before you. If this were going to happen to me, I'd have liked all the trimmings. All I had time for was *God, don't let me die now*. I clutched the gutter; it came apart in my hand and fell with me. The driveway pavement flew up to meet us. Didn't feel a thing when I hit. That's good, right?

In the ambulance, a paramedic—sexy as Montgomery Clift—placed a cigarette between my lips, then lit it, despite the oxygen tank right there. I was a mummy in my sheet, all eyes. He brushed a strand of hair off my forehead. That's when I felt the blood on it, already caking. That would be our close-up. He was perfect for me—attentive, experienced, someone who'd treat me right. He rescued me in a Rescue Unit—how many girls can say that? I could feel the ambulance going fast, but no siren.

"Why no siren?" I whispered, strangely unable to raise my voice.

"You want the siren?" the paramedic said, leaning close. "You can have the siren."

He signaled to the driver.

The driver stuck his head out his window and yelled, "Whoo! Whoo! Whoo!"

This is worth it, right? It's worth the money to show-off your body, if only to the sun. It's worth the look on Beverix's face when he sees me in this sexy number. The bathing suit is me. The saleslady said, "You won't be seeing yourself coming and going in *this*." Summer in a body cast in the psych ward was the last thing on my mind. No pain. I could smoke. I could flirt with this heart-throb moving the cigarette in and out of my lips with my every shallow breath.

"Make it last, sweetheart," he said like Bogie.

# ALL THE KNIVES IN EMERGENCY

Stupid to have an accident on a national holiday, the emergency room strewn with the bloody proof of why you shouldn't fight with guns or knives. Someone sewed up my scalp wound painlessly. Someone else cut the swimsuit open, the surgical scissors swerving, my breasts tumbling out like a trashy bodice-ripper. Behind a filmy curtain I swam in and out of an etherized dream, punctuated by a nurse now and then, popping in to ask me what day or year it was.

"Why are you asking *me*? Ask another nurse. Or an orderly." But that is why I remember Memorial Day, 1965 so well.

Hours passed. A nurse offered to call my mother, which hadn't occurred to me. It wasn't until Mother was there and they unfurled me like a jellyroll from the gurney to the X-ray table that all the knives in Emergency stabbed me in the back. Mother white as gauze.

The ward looked like a hospital scene from every war movie I'd ever seen—men groaning and calling *Nurse!* or *Mother*. Whenever I swam to the surface of the Demerol sea, Mother was there, vigilant as statuary.

"Don't worry," she said. "You're not staying here. Someone in a semi-private will be discharged any minute."

I understood she didn't want anyone to visit me in the ward and think the Diamonds couldn't afford a semi. She whispered *psssst pssst psst*, coaxing me to pee. My mother was regal, not the sort of person who imitates the sound of bodily functions in public. She did that for me.

Waking out of a swoon, I saw the Feins.

"You came too soon," Mother told them. "She'll be in a semi any minute."

"We rushed right over as soon as we heard," Mrs. Fein said.

"You look like death warmed over," my boss said to me.

I'd never heard that expression before. Even under the circumstances, I loved a new way of saying something.

"Remember that for me," I breathed to Mother.

# THE PERSIAN RUG

The semi: Neither I nor my roommate could turn our heads to see each other. She was in traction.

A nurse said to me in a friendly manner, "Lie perfectly still, unless you want to be a hunchback."

We opened our mouths like birdies when the dinner fork appeared in the ceiling sky. At night, waiting for the sleeping pills to kick in, we hummed Stephen Foster: *borne like a vapor on the summer air.*

My friend Michael Dreyfuss came to visit. I asked him to describe the floor. We take for granted there's something under our feet until our toes are pointing up.

"It's covered wall-to-wall with a sumptuous Persian rug," he said.

"Remarkable for a hospital, and this isn't even a private room. An intricate pattern—labyrinths, tendrils, sinuosity—the usual fifteenth-century–Asian mentality."

I'd forgotten to warn him not to make me laugh. Laughter jiggles the spine.

"Red is the main color—a good choice to hide the blood—"

Choked peals of hilarity raked my body. Orderlies rushed him away. I heard him protesting down the hall, "But I didn't even tell her about the fringe!"

*Sandy Diamond*

# THE CAST

Once the nurse feeding me dropped the fork on the floor and I screamed—separate from my will, I tell you—as though it were my hair or the pillow screaming, not me. The nurse stood there, not daring to slap or shake me. My roommate jerked instinctively to help, ramming her limbs against their bounds. *Her* scream shut me up at last. Why couldn't I bear for a fork to fall? Was it me hurtling from the roof? How can a person be a fork? We both fell, that's all I know.

Someone yelled, "Get her out of here!" Someone else called, "No empty beds in Psychiatric." They wheeled me into a storeroom with a door that shut. No intercom. No rug. The door opened to reveal an intern with a hypodermic.

"I'm not a mental patient," I informed him. "I have a fractured lumbar. You're not supposed to jiggle my spine."

I didn't blame him; he had his orders. I blamed the second intern with the second needle.

"I already had the shot. Ask the other guy." I'd never had a double Thorazine before. I could hear my teeth cracking. Someone set a washcloth in my mouth. They knew they'd made a mistake.

There was a window. That's how I knew it was dusk when Herb came. The night—ignorant of beauty and pain—wheeled its stars above the sound and unsound alike. When I could make out the pigeonholed instruments in their plastic sleeves, I understood Herb and I had talked all night, that he'd given up his sleep for me. I thought, *I should try harder to live in this world*. Morning, a new day, when someone was going home and there would be room for me on the psych ward, where Herb would protect me.

*Through this veil, a faraway sound—a bell! Mother's cowbell calling Dinner! Dinner. We retrace our steps like children guided by crumbs—down*

*No-Touch Hill past rabbis chanting, Toe out. Trilliums calling, "Join us." And the gnarled horseradish asking, "Hey, kids, is it Passover yet?" Past springhouse, past orchard to home. Home exists and we could go there—the cowbell of home.*

Semi-private room. Nurses galore. My fellow citizens visited one by one. They were crazed, but they could walk. One young man from a prominent Cleveland family told me he'd broken his back the year before, implying I wasn't all that special.

"The cast drove me crazy," he said. "I broke it off by hitting it against a doorknob whenever no one was looking." High on his shoulders rode a peaked hump.

This is how it's done: Still as a bone, you are suspended between two tables—did you know that? They wind gauze around and around you like some children's game. *Wake up now, wake up now*, I told myself. Nothing in life had prepared me for this. In spite of everything, it was comical: doctors stirring a pot of plaster, their sleeves rolled up like auto mechanics. But it was my chassis on the rack. The warmth of the plaster caught me by surprise, tears springing to my eyes.

"Not much longer," they said, thinking it was pain.

But it was the comfort.

"*Voilà!*" one said. "Are you ready for your French designer gown?"

"Plaster of Paris! Get it?"

Next they wanted me to walk. Strapped to a machine that tilted me by degrees, I learned how to be vertical again. An aide held a bowl of ice near my mouth, popped me a cube whenever I looked green at the gills. When I was upright enough, I saw a ten-year-old girl gripping one oar in a little boat.

Where was her other arm? My eyes moved from the knob of her shoulder to her face. She was beaming.

"Look at me!" she cried. "I'm rowing!"

# ERROL FLYNN'S TEETH

I demanded a dentist examine my teeth, ran my tongue over the Thorazine cracks. I had so much to say, there wasn't room for all my teeth in my jaw. They shoved each other for space like over-eager comedians with no straight man. Teeth rooted in the mouth inches from the brain—if teeth are crooked, how can the mind escape deformity?

Mother said, "When teeth overlap, it gives the impression of an unbecoming appetite." That's me alright. She said a mouthful. To empty my mouth, the dentist had pulled four permanent teeth. Not the wisdom teeth, yanked long ago. I mean the teeth next to them. Those teeth weren't innocent enough to put under my pillow for fairies to come in the night, leaving quarters because what comes out of your mouth has value.

The tongue is a crocodile crouched below the enameled arc of biting. How do tongue and teeth negotiate their borders—the teeth immovable, glossy and hard, the tongue muscular, waggy? Growing up, it was either "Hold your tongue"—my parents could see my words on the tip of my tongue—or "Bite your tongue"—the teeth getting the upper hand when it was too late, when something unmentionable slipped out, something no one wanted to hear and didn't believe.

One day, my longtime dentist, Dr. Bob, appeared. Dr. Bob, who looked like Errol Flynn, played opera while he worked, got tears in his eyes when the pain came through his patient's Novocain. He'd visited New York when I was at Columbia and took me to see Olivier on Broadway in *The Entertainer*—was that just four years ago? This gallant, gentle, precise man in my psych ward shining his little light in my crazy mouth, looking like he was about to cry again.

He said, "I don't see anything wrong."

"I *heard* them crack. Look again. Did they tell you to pretend it's my imagination? I'm really disappointed in you—I thought you'd tell me the truth. I can feel the cracks with my tongue!"

He who crunched silver in the holes of my sugar-loving teeth, who gave me the most glamorous Broadway experience of my life. Who had made inquiries—I heard later—of his social circle—which overlapped my parent's social circle—if I might be a suitable wife for him. Who put his instruments back into their carrying case and backed out the door—his back stooped from bending over twenty years of open mouths—Dr. Bob, Dr. Bob, I'm sorry, his eyes evading my eyes, murmuring, "Goodbye now, Sandy." He meant forever.

# MARILYN MONROE

"Cast...too tight...can't breathe," I accused the doctors, those smug dressmakers. Finally, a guy leaning over my bed with a saw.

"Just hold still, little lady," he said.

What else had I been doing for the merry month of June?

"Done...this...before?" I said in my Marilyn Monroe whisper.

"Talking makes the chest move," he said. "The neck bone's connected to the breast bone."

My downcast voice reminded me of Marilyn Monroe in *The Misfits*. In the opening credits, puzzle pieces—that you can see don't fit—slowly sail by each other, the holes like mouths. Montgomery Clift's ravaged face rearranged. Someone says to Monroe's character, *Whatever happens to anyone happens to you*—an injured rabbit, the wild horses trying to escape.

He carved out a lower neckline for my Parisian frock. Too late I realized there would be less cast to support me. But these are the choices we have to make in life: to heal properly or to breathe. At least now it was easier to get scratched.

"Scratch me! Scratch me!" I'd call out to footsteps in the hall.

With a bit of cotton fastened to a stick, a nurse would reach into the top or bottom of the cast and scratch me, never hard enough. The other patients didn't have a scratcher—only me. They had to scratch their own crazy selves. Someone brought me pistachio nuts. Nurses pried open the shells and popped the nutmeats into my mouth.

Dr. Weiss said, "Life is like pistachio nuts, some parts easy to get at, some hard."

I like people to say things like that when I'm actually eating the metaphor.

# A BLUE SAILING SHIP

Miss Lovelace, the kindest nurse—they were all kind in Psych—looked at me for a long time, then came real close and stroked my cheek.

"You seem to be growing a beard," she whispered. She held a mirror to my face.

"I'm a man! I'm a man!" I croaked. How many people get this opportunity? In my previous life, I shaved every few days. It had been a month since the fall. Dr. Weiss appeared, clean-shaven as usual.

"You never cease to amaze me," he drawled.

"I look more like Freud than you do!"

"Would that you took after him in other ways. An aide is coming to give you a shave."

"Can't stand the competition, eh?"

A big Black man with a can of Barbasol, a thermos of steaming water, and a razor loomed over my bed. I had to make him like me.

"I know lots of Blacks," I said.

"Good for you. Don't talk."

"Or do you prefer 'Negro'?"

"I prefer you don't talk."

"The kitchen at the Tasty Shop is full of you guys."

"Just so you know, it won't be my fault if I cut your throat."

He had a light touch, his dark fingers stretching my lonely jaw. I'd get a few words in while he was rinsing the razor.

"LeRoy is the head cook. He always has a ciggy hanging off his lip. Once, I saw an ash fall into the *soup du jour*."

"Don't move."

"He saw that I saw. He winked at me."

"Good for him."

"Am I the first girl you ever shaved?" I realized I liked getting shaved, someone touching my face. Paying close attention to me. I found I could stop talking if I really had to. At the time, I was on guard, but thinking about it later I remembered I felt less lonely. I also liked the beard. I'm not hard to please. Actually, I'm a very agreeable person.

"Did they tell you I was crazy?"

"This is the psych ward. I figured it out."

"They've got me in a body cast and I'm jumping out of my skin."

"Everyone has problems," he said.

*The smell of the shaving cream reminded me of Daddy shaving when I was a child. A blue sailing ship, little red flags flying from the masts. The waves were drawn in ringlets like how my hair would look if God had seen fit to give me curls instead of giving them to Michael, who didn't even want them.*

# BEVERIXING

Beverix called me at the psych ward. He was almost finished with grading finals. He was coming. The nurse held the phone to my mouth. Any day now. No primping in a body cast. The name Beverix sounded like a prescription. I passed the hours Beverixing myself.

Michael Dreyfuss visited again. He sat in the visitor's chair. I was so happy to see him, the smile was still on my face when he said, "Beverix is dead." The cast tightened. There was no air. My Beverix is coming, he said so, I heard his voice.

"He'd had a heart attack before. The doctor said no strenuous activity. He didn't want me to tell you."

I'd never seen Michael sad before. He loved to laugh. I thought: *This isn't happening. Michael is such a joker—remember the rug?* Now his head was bowed, his hands hiding his face, his rock musician hair shaking. Beverix was thirty-three. That isn't fair, even for God.

"He died in bed. Alone."

"Alone?" I promised I wouldn't ask for love and I loved him. How did God interpret this? Was it okay for me to love as long as no one loved me back?

# NINA SIMONE

"Victrola," I panted to Mother. "Nina...Simone." With its square box and plastic handle, the Victrola looked like a little suitcase. But I wasn't going anywhere. I'd be half sleep in my hollow log, basting in Ohio's humidity. Nina Simone's husky voice reached into the husk of me:

*My baby don't care for shows*
*My baby don't care for clothes*
*My baby just cares for me—*

When the last song on side A was over, the needle slithered about until someone came and set it at the beginning of "My Baby" again, played over and over like the administration of an intravenous drip. Nina in my bloodstream, Nina in my veins. At the time, I didn't analyze why it was "My Baby Just Cares for Me" and not "Little Girl Blue" or "You'll Never Walk Alone." Now I think when you're manic in a body cast, pensive won't do. *You'll Never Walk Alone*—I didn't know if I'd walk, period. I didn't want to think about that, I didn't want to be blue. I wanted someone to just care for me. Not a doctor, not a nurse, but a man so mine I could call him *baby*. In the song, the list of celebrities and amusements he didn't care for delighted me. All he wanted was me. And all I wanted was him. At some point, Nina stopped singing about her baby and started singing about me:

*I wonder what's wrong with baby—*

She cared for me. Even though I was a mental case and medical students from Case Western Reserve appeared in my room and asked me unreasonable questions, she sang and sang until the music—seeping under the cast—coaxed the broken bones back together. She sang and they knit, she was the knitting needle clicking, clicking, the piano lusty and spry, her voice dusky and pure.

# THE TURTLE

One day I heard a foreign language in the hall. Yiddish. Unbelievable. My doctor's voice. By then, we had been together for six years and I was calling him by his first name—*Herb*. I couldn't hear the other half of the conversation. To speak Yiddish out loud in public is to say, "I am a Jew." I was afraid and he was unafraid, the youngest head of Psychiatric at any hospital in the United States. Miss Lovelace told me so. Finally, he came into my room.

"What's with the Yiddish?" I pounced.

He said, "My patient is eighty-five years old, profoundly depressed. ECT will give him back his life. He needs to hear this in his native tongue."

"He's so old. It won't work. What if he dies?"

Herb said, "*I must be cruel only to be kind.*"

"Why not skip the middleman and be kind in the first place? I could die inside this mausoleum and no one would notice."

"We'd notice we hadn't heard from you after two minutes."

"By then, it would be too late to resuscitate me."

"Sandy, I hear that you're afraid."

"Mother's back hurts. She doesn't bend down to kiss me anymore."

"That must make you feel even more alone."

"Everyone loves you—what do you know about loneliness?"

Herb was quiet for a long time. He got up and closed the door, looking back at me.

Finally, he spoke slowly in a low voice.

"When I was four, I had a pet turtle. He lived in a box by my bed. We played together. I caught flies to feed him. We told each other our secrets. Then one day when I tickled him with a blade of grass, he didn't move. We didn't know why he died. That's when I learned about loneliness."

I pictured Herb at four. He would've been chubby, adorable. His personal life had never been part of our conversations. I knew this much: to be mentally ill was inseparable from loneliness. You are separated from your own mind. Miss Lovelace told me psychiatrists all over the country wanted to know about shock for the aged. She said Herb's patient was discharged a happy man.

---

The day after the cast came off, I was released. That proves I wasn't crazy, only broken. "They cut it in two halves *like a clamshell*," an aide said and a nurse said, "Doesn't a clam refer to a closed-mouthed person?"

We all laughed and I felt for the first time since the fall that I was a real person, normal, just like them. Everyone signed the cast, the aides writing risqué puns along the edges.

My parents wanted me to stay with them but even in my steel corset, I needed to be back in my Surrey Road apartment. Needed to see my paintings, my books, my cat. The whitewashed brick wall of love. I was told: No bending. I propped the cast in a corner of my studio, talked to it. Sometimes I wished I could crawl back into the cast and a nurse would come and pick up all the stuff I'd dropped on the floor. And Beverix would glide down the stairs and make love to me.

## HUNCHBACK

A few years after the fall, I couldn't stand up at the easel anymore. I didn't know enough to exercise, build myself up. Or maybe the doctors had told me and I didn't hear. Or maybe I heard and didn't listen, didn't believe them, didn't believe the body had anything to do with me, the real me. All I cared about was The Muse. She had to keep talking to me.

The neglected spine gradually telescoped down eight inches, pushed out a miscreant hump. My neck ached from looking up at people. The first time a tall man—an Oakland politician—bent on one knee to talk to me, I was overwhelmed by this simple act of thoughtfulness. He had *my* vote. This was the time when people's backpacks slammed into the hump, the sweet toes of babies backward in their carriers wiggled in my face. I thought: Any day now, someone will ask me, *Where is your tin cup? Where's your monkey?*

*Sandy Diamond*

# AN INEXTINGUISHABLE LONGING

Healers were sent to me. David—who studied with Moshe Feldenkrais in Israel—believed in increments. One day, I felt a door slide open in my spine. Feldenkrais visited San Francisco, worked on me. Excruciating, but for the first time, I drove home across the Bay Bridge weeping with joy—no pain. The pain returned, but that bridge ride—that brief suspension of my accursed shadow—fed my hope that I could lift my son Gabriel again, could fling and whirl him and throw him into a beanbag. That I could be someone else.

David put me in a body movement class. The floor, gaudy with youth in emerald and ruby leotards. I laid my poor back on the wealthy floor. Self-pity sprawled like a drunk in my lap. David saw I wasn't moving to the serenity tape. He wove through the jewels to the carpet frayed by my tears and told me a story as though it was bedtime and I a weary child.

It was Moshe's story from The War. He and other Jews hid in a house in London, quiet as bones in the bombing night. Several refugees were pianists and there was a piano, its every daylight hour parceled out among them. When darkness fell, the lid descended even if they were in the middle of Mozart. I'd have thought that when another pianist was smuggled in, the others would give up a fraction of their playing time, but that's not what happened. Perhaps they'd already given up all they could bear. The newcomer told Moshe she had to practice or she would go mad. He saw the spirit that gave the slip to Nazis wilt like cut flowers whose stems no longer reach the water.

But then one morning she was radiant.

"Last night I played."

"You can't have played! We'd have heard you. And the Germans!"

That night, he watched from behind the black-out drape as she crept in the darkness to the piano. Despite the rags she escaped in, she sat as though wearing a formal gown, briefly arranging a long skirt that wasn't there. Her fingers slid back the black lid and stretched over the ivory. And began to play. Moshe could tell it was Chopin from the passionate flight of her hands that spoke of an inextinguishable longing for homeland, hands that reached like a flower to water, hands that flew all night just above the keys.

"So, you see," said David, "just do the best you can."

# THE HUNCHBACK OF NOTRE DAME

While the film was being shot, Hitler marched into Czechoslovakia. Charles Laughton as Quasimodo turned on the pillory, his face inhuman, a monstrous approximation of man. He slowly turned as though away from humanity itself. Despite his saving the day with the boiling oil he pours on the Parisians storming the cathedral door and the swinging rope with which he rescues Esmeralda—*Sanctuary! Sanctuary!*—she rides off with the handsome poet. Victor Hugo didn't do happy endings. Quasimodo leaned on a gargoyle, less grotesque than he, and delivers his last line:

"Why wasn't I made of stone like thee?"

The camera backed away until he was indistinguishable from the façade of Notre Dame.

## THE JOURNEY INSIDE THEM

I remembered people like me when I was a child. At the Tasty Shop, the refugees wore humps inside their black coats. Bowed over misty bowls of soup, they looked like a mountain range, their journey inside them. I imagined the displaced people flocked at harbors where not enough boats would sail to America.

Since everyone had a number, someone called out, "*Hunchbacks first!*"

All afternoon, they sipped hot tea from a tall glass. They held a lump of sugar between their back teeth and waved the bread baskets for more braided rolls, more challah, as though—Mother said—what manners they had over there didn't come with them. The waitresses knew not to give them the rush even as Gladys, Charlotte, and Marge billowed and spread the white dinner tablecloths, hoping the breeze would reach "the Old Country," as we called their tables, and they'd take a hint. But our little ghetto was beyond hints.

The one we named The Scholar always disputed his check as though it were The Talmud. Cashier, waitress, and scholar stood, poking their pencils at the pale-lined paper that said, *Thank you for coming*. If anyone was going to be cheated, it wouldn't be him. Once the Old Country was up in arms about the thickness of a blintz. Mrs. V, the Hungarian cook, stormed out from the kitchen—Gladys or Marge must have told her what was going on—and loomed over the grievance committee staring up at her. As big as two chopping blocks on piano legs, in such a huff she raised her rolling pin, her apron vast and snowy as Siberia. "Shame on you!" she said. She'd been through what they'd been through.

Half a century later, the restaurant's gone, along with Mother, Father, Mrs. V, our crooked-back customers. Their commentary about our incomparable borscht, our latkes light as angels, seem to me now a ritual to keep the ghosts of their dead from envy. Did Nature armor them with humps to stave off the thrusts of history? Or did these humps spring fullfledged when a guard tapped them on their bony backs, grinning, *Not yet?* Do they store provisions there for crossing their private Sinai's? Are such deformities meant to be straightened? Are they not testaments—bulging medals of grace—like bread rising misshapen from the wrong recipe, the bent staff of life?

Ah, Quasimodos of my parents' mercy, let me be a girl again holding on to a sweet. For who's to say a hump isn't a good thing—all our pain knotted in one bundle behind us, *kenahora*.

*To An Insane Degree*

# THE JEW-HATER'S TROLLEY, 1946

After Hebrew School one day, Michael and I stood on the trolley tracks on Mayfield Road because the trolley man wouldn't stop at the synagogue. The trolley man hated Jews even though the war was over. The week before, we had to walk one mile uphill to the bus terminal because he clanged right past us.

"This time," Michael said, "we're not walking. He's supposed to stop."

It was common knowledge in my family that the first-born gets the most brains. Michael said to me he wouldn't let the trolley hit us. Our oxfords slipped on the shiny rails. I clutched my Hebrew books, which may not touch the ground.

"If Hebrew touches the ground," Miss Zemetkin had said, "you must pick up the black letters twisting to escape detection and kiss them."

5:10. The Jew-hater's trolley was right on time. The rails' vibrations *wah wah* up my legs. I was shaking like those wooden dolls that dance a jig when a stick hits by their feet, those do-with-me-as-you-will shameless puppets of shaking.

The spokes of the cowcatcher were visible now, the train dangling from its overhead wire—

*Blessed art thou, king of the universe...*

Its clanging bells, the honking cars—blood beating in my ears.

I'm clutching the back of Michael's coat praying, "Listen to me, trolley. Stop now!" I saw passengers inside the trolley gesturing, *Away, away!*

*God of our fathers...*

A woman's open mouth formed a perfect O. Black letters circled the train's iron face: spelling CLEVELAND TRANSIT SYSTEM—the last words I'll ever read—

*Hear, oh Israel...* the trolley man's face masked in the glare of the sun setting on his windshield. The one-eyed light will shine on our bodies torn from their spines. Who will pick them up and kiss them, *oh holy one?*

Fifteen feet away from us, the trolley—screeching—ground to a halt. My legs were numb. Michael pulled me up the stairs, dropped our fares into the changer without looking at the trolley man. But I looked. He stared straight ahead as though we were still out there, waiting for the 5:10, on the tracks of the Lord.

# BEYOND REPAIR

My trusty VW Bug needed servicing. I left it at Beyond Repair off San Pablo Avenue—living in Berkeley then—and walked to the bus stop at Big O Tires. A man waiting there gave me the look-over.

"I never made it with a hunchback before," he said, a cigarette moving with his lips. "I wonder what it'd be like to make love to you."

So now I was a freak, unmistakable even in this city of freaks. Actually, I liked it when someone acknowledged my hump instead of sneaking glances. He reminded me of the child on Telegraph Avenue last year who cried, "Look, Mommy, a dwarf!"

I too looked where his finger was pointing, somewhere behind me. He meant me. So, I thought, *Now I'm a dwarf.* It takes some getting used to. The mother grabbed his irrevocable finger, but he knew what he saw. All those years Mother said, *Sit up straight, toe out,* how could she see my back bulging like wings badly folded, fused to the spine like a sculpture from the *Salon des Refusés*?

Hey, I know I'm not the only one. I've seen my hunched comrades skulking about town. They always wear coats—black coats even in summer—so you think a scarf is bunched up in there, a really big scarf, or the hanger. And when they take the coat off, the hump will come with it, like a detachable lining. And the body will be undefiled.

*Sandy Diamond*

# LITTLE SISTER, 1969

When depression slammed her into despair, Dianne was a social worker in Long Beach, twenty-six. Methodical, she left her last two paychecks on her dresser, endorsed to me. Stuffed towels in the window cracks. Got down most of a vial of Elavil.

"Were you in anguish?" I asked, decades later when she told me.

"No, I felt nothing."

Blew out the pilot light, rested her head on the open oven door. Little sister. And then, she told me she'd thought of me, thought of Stan and Beverix.

"I couldn't cause you the pain of another death," she said.

Although they were dead, Stan and Beverix saved her. And that is all we can do in this life—believe we can't pass on the hurt. Dianne never knew Stan or Beverix, yet they lived in her. She closed the oven door.

*For there is no friend*
*like a sister*
*In calm or stormy weather;*
*To cheer one on the tedious way,*
*To fetch one if one goes astray,*
*To lift one if one totters down*
*To strengthen whilst one stands.*
—Christina Rossetti, "Goblin Market"

Dianne flew to Ohio to take me back to California with her. We'd drive cross-country so I could feel myself leaving the old life behind as she had done before me. But how to leave my nieces? I adored Michael's four little girls.

Dianne said, "You can stay here and be an aunt or you can go to California and have a child of your own."

*To An Insane Degree*

Mother said, "If you get in trouble, you'll be too faraway for us to help."

I hadn't had a breakdown in four years, had money saved up from selling two canvases. But she was afraid for me. Once you've screamed, "I'll kill you!" no one trusts you.

*Sandy Diamond*

# THE EGYPTIAN BOOK OF THE DEAD

We were the Diamond Girls taking turns behind the wheel of my Simca on the I-Can-Dream-Can't-I? Freeway, yelling *bon mots* from *Portnoy's Complaint* louder than traffic amid peals of hilarity. I was crossing the continent to have a child of my own. You could fit four Ohios in California. It was a mathematical certainty I'd get my way. I wasn't looking for The Lasting Love of a Man anymore. I was looking for Baby Diamond. And if the *Egyptian Book of the Dead* was right, the soul of the baby was looking for my womb. But first, like a fairy tale, I worked for three years at entry-level jobs, holding the vision of the baby I would get at the end. We laughed all the way to L. A.

# RED LACE

Just before I left, I was in my parents' bedroom, watching them dress for a dance. Dad in a black suit, dapper as his wedding picture, Mother in strapless red lace, a matching shrug draped on her vanity stool.

"Sam," Mother breathed, "zip me up."

I think Dad lived for the chance to zip her up—the only thing she couldn't do herself. My father drawing the zipper up her pretty back was the sexiest thing I remember them doing in front of me.

"What's this?" he said.

Just above the zipper, a dark blot sprawled near her shoulder blade. He guided her hand behind her back to feel it.

She kept the jacket on that night. The melanoma was removed. The doctor said it wouldn't be back.

Sandy Diamond

# MAXIE

My parents, Samuel and Elizabeth, met in 1929. He had to leave his architecture studies at Case Institute, making a living painting signs: *Going Out of Business, Everything Must Go, Final Days.* An aspiring concert pianist, Elizabeth taught piano for fifty cents an hour. Her parents expected her to be someone.

My father's oldest brother was Maxie Diamond, rumored to be Al Capone's man in Cleveland. In the tradition of Italian and Jewish first-born sons of 1920s and '30's American immigrants, Maxie supported the family in the rackets—bootlegger, laundry, cleaner and dryer wars, drawing the line at drugs and prostitution. During Prohibition, he was connected with a syndicate, smuggling large quantities of illicit liquor from Canada. In the book *The Silent Syndicate* my uncle was called the nattiest dresser of the Cleveland Dry Cleaning Mob. In a front-page newspaper photo of Max, he is in his natty fedora, handcuffed between federal agents. Elizabeth's parents forbid her to bring *that gangster's brother* into their house.

Abraham and Minnie said, "We didn't come to America for our daughter to marry a gangster." I still have my parents' love letters in the candy box from the 1920s.

*CLEVELAND PLAIN DEALER, JANUARY 10, 1933:*
  RACKETEER MAXIE DIAMOND IN CAR DUCKS AS SHOTS POUR IN ASSAILANTS SPEED PAST IN AUTO, LIGHTS OUT
  Maxie Diamond, 36, narrowly escaped death from underworld bullets last night in what police say is a continuation of the city's dry cleaning war. Diamond ducked down in the front seat of his automobile just as two revolver bullets from a passing car crashed through the glass in the left front door of his Lincoln sedan.

The shots were aimed high and low, one for the head, the other for the heart. Had Diamond been seated in the normal position at the wheel he would have received the bullets as intended.

[A 5" x 4" photo of the car window shows the two bullet holes ringed by shattered glass]

If this had happened, the city would have been relieved of Diamond, known to police as a bad character.

1929, Girl of My Dreams, Today I fished in Lovesick Lake.

Love Letters on birch bark. Each line of script flows to the edge of the page as though no time to lift the pen, as though handwriting itself would woo her—the high-looped ascenders of desire.

## MADAME BUTTERFLY

1930. The New York Metropolitan Opera was coming to town. The Cleveland Press ran a contest—a puzzle of the divas' faces to be unscrambled, obscure arias to be identified. In the borders of the contest application form—a skill my father had learned touching up the secondhand Seagram's and Beefeater labels on Maxie's home brew. My mother's beau painted miniature stage settings with a brush, Daddy told me, of four hairs: Rudolfo weeping at the dying Mimi's bedside; Madame Butterfly clutching her son to her flowered kimono a tiny ship receding in the distance; and the horses of *Aida*. The prize was two seats for each gala performance. He entered the contest in Elizabeth's name. She won. Her picture was on the front page, above the fold.

Abraham and Minnie received congratulations for their daughter's triumph.

"After all, a man isn't his brother," they said. An aunt told me the sweethearts borrowed every stitch they wore to the opera. They held their heads high in the gilded splendor of Severance Hall amidst the Tafts and Bings.

# BOOTLEG MASSACRE, 1930

Maxie got a tip that a shipment of Canadian moonshine was going to be highjacked.

"Don't take this trip," he ordered, then begged his partners. They didn't listen. In a spectacular double-crossing shootout, two Harry's, a Hymie, and an Al were wiped out. When the assassins and the press realized Maxie was not among the violently departed, his escape was viewed as voodoo. He had vanished from the scene into thin air. He became *The Man Who Wasn't There*. His partners gone, he fled the country. He made a deal with the government, joining the Army for four years to come back a free man from past misdeeds. He loved America and served with pride.

# ELIOT NESS AND PRESIDENT ROOSEVELT

*Cleveland Plain Dealer. October 1936*:
HONEST MAN, SAYS DIAMOND OF NESS

Maxie Diamond walked into Central Police Station yesterday and expressed a wish to meet Safety Director Eliot Ness, whom he called "an honest man."

He also picked President Roosevelt to win in the coming election.

He refuted rumors that he had been dumped into Lake Erie the year before. His boat had started to leak—a rumor had him encased in a concrete block and fed to the fishes. Looking like an *Esquire* fashion photo in a well-pressed brown suit, a dark brown snapped-brim hat, and a dashing checked tan topcoat, Diamond puffed a long black cigar. "I know Mr. Ness is a swell guy because you can't buy him for a cigar or any amount of cash."

# SAN FRANCISCO DONUTS, 1969

I became an accounting clerk in an insurance office for high-risk clients. Not bad drivers like you'd think—but celebrities framed by con artists who'd fake an accident and sue the stars for all they were worth. I was furious to see that Joan Baez was paying an exorbitant premium, although her driving record was faultless.

When I applied for this job, I thought, *It's just numbers. My mind will be free.* Instead, every day, I raged at the institutionalized injustice. It was weird because it was the rich who were getting ripped off, but I couldn't help it—I hated the con men. Forcing Joan Baez to dent your car was like war: the innocent got hurt.

Market Street was lined with homeless men, thanks to Reagan closing the state's mental hospitals. There was so much to be accountable for, stuff you can't add up on a calculator. My turn to go for donuts, which meant my turn to feed the bag lady.

She informed me on my first donut run Third and Market was her beat. "Who doesn't know what's in a pink cardboard box tied with string?"

The block was too long to go around to avoid her. I learned to order an extra one for her. Once, I had the bakery girl put the bag lady's donut—jelly, my favorite too—in a separate bag.

The bag lady said, "No way, white girl. I want to pick."

Well, I guess I would too if I was her. I never could get the string back on. Later, it occurred to me it was real ladylike of her to take just one. Her grimy fingers hovered over the quivering box as though she were tasting each one in her mind. What would I have done if she'd taken two? Or six? Or all? Fight? Please. I was spineless as custard, as jimmies, as string.

Outside the entrance to my building, a cluster of amputees strapped to their rollered platforms bummed passersby for change. They knew people had change because the newspaper racks were right there. Some had crudely lettered pieces of cardboard that said *Vet*. One day, without warning, a man rolled from the wall and grabbed the hem of my dress.

"No! Stop!" I screamed.

My fellow Americans stepped off the curb to avoid the legless man attached to me—hand over hand, pulling himself up my one good dress. The weight of his wheeling apparatus, his dead weight. I could smell the wool under my arms turning to rot. I hated the legless men, I hated myself in that not-me-at-all–job-interview dress that turned out to be so climbable. Why didn't I just give him a donut in the first place? That requires fast thinking, not my forte.

## MISTRESS OF PEONIES

We didn't know about secondhand smoke then. I had smoked at home behind my closed door. The smoke sneaked under the door and found Mother. The doctors removed a lung.

I called her by different names in my mind—Mumsy or Mama or *Leah Malke*, her Hebrew name that meant "beautiful queen"—so Death wouldn't recognize her. This is not who you want, Death, not *ma mere*. Death, you can't have her, she's ours—mistress of peonies on the black satin Story & Clark baby grand. Braider of hair that fell into three strands on its own as soon as it saw her coming.

"Why don't you play the piano?" I asked Mother more than once.

"I don't have time to practice."

One day, when no one else was around, she told me to go to the basement and close the door.

"Why? The laundry's all folded."

"Just do what I say for once. Skedaddle."

I went to the basement and sat on the first step with the door open a crack.

After a while, I heard sounds like the waterfall tumbling and climbing up again and again but a sound wetter than water. If only I could make those, I would open all the doors and windows in the whole house. I would play so loud, Tomma could hear it half a mile away, the apple trees on Old Mill Road could hear amazed, for God—deaf to so much—could hear. Then He'd have to send us an honest night manager so Daddy wouldn't have to stay at the Tasty Shop through dinner, so Mother'd have time to practice after her kids were fed and in bed at a decent hour.

It was still summer. Give her more time, more time. We stood in the backyard, a rainbow arching over her garden. Pink roses scampered on arbors as though they didn't have a care in the world. It hadn't been raining. We all stood there looking at the tinted transparent sky, not a scientist among us to explain how that could be. God said, *I will be gracious to whom I will be gracious and I will show mercy on whom I will show mercy.* God, why did you put that rainbow over my mother's garden? You know how my parents are—Dad actually believing that four fawns romping outside the breakfast room window meant his four *dear* children would dance at their mother's recovery. Did you make my father the corniest, biggest-hearted man on earth? Are You laughing at us? You knew Mother would take the rainbow as a sign she would get better. If you were going to slay this good woman who kept the Sabbath and all the rest of your damn commandments, why the fucking rainbow?

# BRING THE WAR HOME!

1970. Berkeley Councilman Ron Dellums at the Civic Center, San Francisco:

*Mothers! If the man came to your door and said, 'I've come for your dog—we're taking your poodle,' you'd say, Hell, no! So, when they come for your son, why would you let him go?*

*Sandy Diamond*

# LEVITATING THE PENTAGON

I met a guy who'd been there—helped the exorcized Pentagon levitate. Abbie Hoffman, encircling the building, trying to raise it three hundred feet. In *Armies of The Night*, Norman Mailer wrote:

*In the air The Pentagon would turn orange and vibrate until all evil emissions had fled. At that point the war in Vietnam would end.*

The Pentagon gave the protestors permission to raise the building ten feet. They nixed encirclement, which everyone knows is the source of enchantment.

*"Out, demons, out!"* the hippies chanted.

Later in bed, my peacenik said, "I don't want to exaggerate. We just got that sucker up off its foundation."

I loved his modesty. How I wanted him then, wanted the Pentagon to unmoor inside me. His finger traced a map of the campaign on my body. The pentacle of power was my belly, its atrium my navel. The South Parking lot, of course, was where he was about to demonstrate the newly famous slogan: *Make Love, Not War*.

Where were the sheets, under me no more? Where the pillow of desire? From the Army-Navy surplus bedroll, the Pentagon exorcist and I rose—not to the ceiling, not to the window—just high enough for lamplight to glow in the space between us and the unmysterious world.

# THE SALON OF THE LORD

*Once, when I was seven or eight, Mother sat in the metal rocking chair in the backyard, letting the sun dry her waist-length hair. I crept up behind her. A breeze lifted her fragrant, damp hair, tickling my face. I opened my mouth. Did she know I was tasting her hair, that I wanted to be her?*

Once, in better days, I was at the cash register, Mother chatting up the Tasty Shop lunch line. Someone admired Mother's silver-streaked, twin-crested hair.

"Mrs. D, where do you get your hair done?"

Mother laughed. "In the salon of the Lord."

Well, *that* salon's out of business. The long black summertime hair that I tried to eat long ago fell out. Bald or in the wig—which was more shocking? She teased Dad he'd taken up with a brunette.

# NIGHTIES

Mother was propped up with pillows in her marriage bed, wearing the white gown with lace shoulders I'd given her. In an old nightie too thin for winter, I kissed her unfamiliar cheek goodnight.

"Give me your nightie in the morning," she said.

"You want *this?*"

"The lace is falling off. Bring the sewing box too."

"Mother, *I'll* do it. You need to rest."

Inside I was saying, "Mother, you're dying. Don't you understand? The days of mending are over. I'll put your gown under my pillow and dream of you. Or cry all night. You can't mend my nightie."

But she did. I watched her grasshopper fingers poke the needle into the worn nylon until the lace was restored. It was her last chance to take care of me.

I bathed *Leah Malke* in December. Washed surgical centipedes and railroad tracks, breathing the smell of inoperable decay. I held her in a towel.

## SHIRLEY TEMPLE UNDRESSED

I was five when Mother gave me my first book of Shirley Temple cutout dolls. Then the War came and I didn't get a new book of paper dolls until I was nine. I rationed the bending of the little tabs that held her clothes to her body in its dainty white slip, waiting for me to dress her. As the War wore on, the tabs thinned and fell off. Shirley became an invalid, lying on my bed, smiling up at me with her famous dimples, tossing her curls as I laid her overalls or pinafores on top of her.

# THE SNIPER

At this time, there was a rooftop sniper downtown, working the stretch between the Ferry Building and my office. I wondered what made him shoot some people and not others. One day, walking to the job, I tossed my purse in the air again and again in a burst of happiness. I should have been eyeing doorways for cover and hugging the walls, the smack of brown leather in my hands. I was asking for it, my foolish heart in his crosshairs. Were I a sniper, I'm just the one who'd piss me off. The third day of the sniper, I was in a funk. Walked to work downcast. The sniper would think: *I'll put that one out of her misery.* I'd make the front page, my photogenic body splayed on the sidewalk, pigeon-toed, a run in my stocking, purse spilling its guts.

# TANGERINES LIKE GOLDFISH

Mother's delicate handwriting, pen barely touching paper with just enough pressure to be legible. Connecting strokes and parts of letters disappeared. I could tell when Dad had darkened her faint lines—he wanted to be sure we understood what she was saying. Most letters started with a weather report, then what flowers were blooming, then food. Who brought what to the house: a sweet potato-pineapple dish, spinach soufflé, Jell-O molds—sections of tangerines swimming in an orange-lime sea like goldfish, which I couldn't bear to see gasping their last on my plate.

As the letters went on, the space between Mother's words widened and Dad's once-wide spaces closed up. Even at the time—when I knew nothing of graphology—I saw Mother distancing from life and Dad trying to fill the gap, trying to hold her in this world. Now he wrote of Bethesda and surgeries instead of Lovesick Lake. He said when they left the hospital for the last time, the other patients were shocked—they thought she was on the staff. Thirty-seven years in the restaurant business, Mr. and Mrs. D couldn't help themselves—they played the host even there in the diner of death.

"Listen to this, Sandy. Mother did the most amazing thing. We were in the elevator at Bethesda for the last time. We didn't speak. I felt her fingers slip into my hand."

"Dad, wives hold their husbands' hands all the time—"

"But Sandy, this was *Mother*."

Sandy Diamond

# MISTAKEN IDENTITY

Broad forehead, square jaw, rimless glasses—my father looked like Glenn Miller. At least from the front. From the side view, you could see he had a hooked nose, and Glenn Miller didn't. When the bandleader's plane went down over the English Channel in 1944, the mistaken identity lived on. The *Cleveland Plain Dealer* ran a story about the phenomenon: *Lost Hero Sightings Epidemic*.

Daddy told me he was lugging a case of Scotch from his Chevy to the Tasty Shop door. Just as he reached the plate glass window—festooned with salamis—he heard a young woman's voice.

"Oh my God, Glenn Miller, it's you!"

He'd always been able to duck behind something when someone "recognized" him. But this time there was no cover.

"Young lady, I am not—"

"I knew you couldn't be dead!"

"Now see here, you're making a big mistake—"

"My husband and I saw you perform at the Palace just before he shipped out."

"Miss, listen, I'm sorry, but—"

"He didn't come back. So that was our last dance."

My father eased the case of spirits against the window's ledge, leaned his hip against the booze. The girl held out a flowered memo pad, a pen attached by a little chain.

"Write *Good Luck to a good soldier*, okay?"

"A kind of terror went through my heart," he told me.

"I knew the famous signature: first and last name joined by a vertical horn-shaped flourish. I kept turning my profile to her, hoping she'd see my hooked nose. But one thing I've learned in the restaurant business—people see what they want to see. Like a sandwich with not enough meat."

# NIXON

One breezy evening on Market Street and Third, a man bought a *Chronicle* from a newspaper rack. A gust from the bay swooped down, seized the paper, and sent it smack into my nearby bag lady.

She tried to fight it off, but Nixon was on her belly yelling, *Bombs Save Lives!*

There was no shortage of photos of Nixon then: he lied and someone took his picture. He was the very picture of lying.

"Get away from me, you lying bastard!" she howled.

The bag lady and Nixon seemed to be dancing together.

I like to think of myself as a compassionate person. Why didn't I help her? Didn't I have the power to turn the situation around? I could have peeled the paper off my fellow citizen. I know what you're thinking: You're thinking, the bag lady is me. It was me screaming on Market Street, San Francisco, the last stop at the end of America. I hadn't been in a hospital for five years. I wasn't supposed to be crazy anymore.

## I'LL SEE YOU AGAIN

Mother insisted Dianne and I go back to our jobs in California. If we learned anything from our parents, we knew you never leave your boss short-handed.

"I'll see you again," she said. "There's time."

When I got the call from home at my office, my new car was hemmed in at the parking lot at three sides. I had to get to the airport to meet Dianne, who would be taking the flight up from LA so we could fly home together. My mother is dying, I told the car she'd bought me, told the cars in my way and no one in sight to tell me what to do, except the vision of emaciated Mother holding a stick with a sign that said, *I'm not going until the last child flies in from the coast.*

I started my car, at first nudging the blocking cars and finally smashing through, sobbing—thinking what I'd say if the police came running, blowing their whistles and screaming, their guns drawn.

Dianne and I got seats on either side of the aisle. We held hands, letting go only when one of us—then both of us—cried enough to have to blow our nose. It's not really letting go if her hand is waiting for mine to return or my hand waits for hers.

## TOO LATE FOR ADDICTION

Before the cancer reached her brain, Mother made it clear she wanted to die at home. She refused the morphine shots as long as possible, saying, "I don't want to be a junkie."

"Can she get addicted?" I whispered to the nurse.

She looked at me as if to see if I were insane or just an idiot. Then whispered back, "She won't live long enough to be addicted."

The nurse held an orange in her left hand, the hypodermic needle in her right.

"This is her hip," she said, looking at me. "The injection goes in like this."

It looked easy enough.

"She'll hardly feel a thing."

She handed me the orange and the needle. My hand began to shake. Is the orange Mother's hip or is Mother's hip the orange? I saw the orange unpeel in my mind as only Mother used to cut it, in one unwinding rind. "Peel me an orange," we kids would say and she would drop what she was doing and peel the orange skin down to its white underwear. Now I will plunge the needle into this piece of fruit. It is not my mother; it is a metaphor. The nurse put her hand over my hand with the hypodermic and squeezed. The needle entered the orange. I screamed.

"For God's sake, Sandy," Dad said.

# THE ORANGE BOWL PARADE

Miami, 1948—the first Rose Bowl Parade since Pearl Harbor. I envied my little brother and sister, perched on our parents' shoulders. I could feel the wanton air, the breeze fragrant with sweet, good-for-you oranges. Michael shimmied up a lamppost to see. Only I couldn't see. A man in a Navy uniform offered a boost.

"I'm from Ohio, too," he said.

Mom and Dad all smiles and thanks.

"Just stay near us, please."

The man took my hand, then lifted me to his U.S. shoulders.

Beautiful ladies glowed briefly, then melted into the night. Invisible men played silvery horns in a pulsing, electric wail—were they ever really there? A lady snapped castanets at a man, his body sleek and spangled, dancing sharp pointy toes into her flounces. They screamed, "Ai-yeee!" and floated away. Orange blossoms wafted heady perfume—over the drifting crowd. A man on a float played a giant orange-shaped piano. I felt fingers in the place you're not supposed to touch. A Punch and Judy show on a float—Punch hits Judy with an orange. The crowd roared with delight. I couldn't see my mother.

"Take me back," I said, my voice finally working.

Judy squeezes an orange over Punch's head. Juice drips from his long nose.

There's Michael on the lamppost. There's Charles and Dianne on our parents' shoulders. The sailor put me down by Mommy and Daddy's feet. I was crying.

"Nothing happened," he said.

# I AM HERE

On the night table between my parents' beds was the lamp they'd had all their marriage. On its parchment shade, an old man astride a camel crossed the desert past dunes and palm trees, around and around, like someone out of *The Arabian Nights*. While the sands of Mother's time ran out.

In the night table cabinet was a Fanny Farmer candy box, shaped like a pirate's treasure chest, inset with cardboard emeralds and rubies. Inside, Mother kept her mementos. As a girl, I studied the hand-painted invitations to a fraternity dance, wedding cards from 1933, and pastel congratulations on the birth of each child. Yellowing newspaper clippings of Mother's piano recitals and scholarships, a sheaf of picture postcards addressed to Mother's maiden name. The Damascus Gate, the ruins of Pompei and Transylvania. Monaco. A wedding cake on the edge of a blue sea.

In crude writing they all said, *I am here. Love, Maxie.*

# ETERNITY

Inch by inch, Dad moved each hanger in her closet, looking for the best dress. He sat on her bed, her moth-green dress in his arms chosen for its high neck, long sleeves, and tiny hand-sewn seed pearls. Forgive us, Mother, that dress was not warm enough for winter. How do you dress for Eternity, Mama? You never told me. She who promised moles were beauty spots, who saved my crayoned valentines, who listened to soap operas while ironing hankies. I think of my father, who sometimes said "ain't," sometimes forgot to call when he was stuck at the Tasty Shop through dinner and we were waiting for him to bring our dinner home, Michael and me hungry at the living room picture window, waiting for headlights turning into our drive from the road.

"Don't make a fuss over me," Mother would have said. "Does everyone have a glass of water and a menu? Whatever you do, dress warm."

A Californian now, I didn't have a winter coat. Dad told me to wear one of Mother's. Her coats, hanging next to his coats in the hall closet. The closet that once kept our childhood snowsuits and mittens on don't-lose-me elastic. Did Mother's coats miss her body slipping into their sleeves? Here was her blue cloth coat with its white, fur-like collar, its whiff of Arpège. Dad asked me to wear my hair up. So that's how I looked at the cemetery where sweet, sad Cousin Joe saw me for the first time in years and cried across the open grave, "Elizabeth!"

## THE QUEEN OF ENGLAND

Once, I saw a picture of the Queen of England in *Life Magazine*. Petite, dark-haired, regal. She looked just like my mother when she dressed up to go out. They even had the same name: Elizabeth. After Mother kissed me goodnight, she went to England to be the English queen. Every morning, she made it back in time to be my Mum again. She was never late. I longed to say to her, "Your majesty." I practiced curtsies in the mirror. Someday, reaching into her closet, she'd take out her shiny crown.

"Don't make things up," Mother used to say.

# REAL LEATHER

"I don't want to leave with your old car always breaking down," Mother had said in the spring. She sent me money for a new VW Bug, an extravagance in our family.

Daddy had said, "That's a lot of money; she should get a used car."

"She doesn't have enough sense to buy a used car," Mother said.

That Bug lasted sixteen years before I sold it to a sailor from the Oakland shipyard who wanted it for parts.

"That's real leather on the steering wheel," I said, trying not to let my voice crack.

"Take it," he said.

But I couldn't—it would have been like robbing a corpse.

## HER BRAIDS

Going through Mother's vanity drawers with Dad, we gathered up her ironed, initialed handkerchiefs—hoping there were enough for each waitress to have one. In the back of a drawer, an envelope. At my touch, something inside moved—her dark braids uncoiling.
  "Why weren't these buried with her?" I asked, anger rising.
  "It doesn't matter now," he said.
  "She would have wanted her hair with her," I said. "I hope you didn't put that damn wig in the coffin!"
  "Calm down, don't talk about it." We were both weeping.
  "If this happens to me"—meaning cancer—"I want my hair with me!" I screamed.
  "Did you say *if?*" he whispered. He meant death.

*Sandy Diamond*

# THE LADIES' ROOM, 1944

Squinting through the crack of the door of the toilet stall, I'd watch the ladies at the Tasty Shop reflected in the mirror. With tiny brushes unscrewed from golden tubes, they drew lips and eyes and lashes, puffed powder from their gleamy compacts, rolled the hand towel machine to a clean spot, and kissed it.

Reaching under their skirts, they yanked their girdles down, ran fingers up the backs of their legs until their seams were straight. Some plucked atomizers from their purses and squeezed the bulb, releasing a mist near their earringed ears, humming, "Pistol Packin' Mama" and "This Is The Army, Mr. Jones." There was always one who bent her leg at the knee like a horse being shoed, spit on two fingers, and rubbed a scuff from her sling-back platform pump. Then she'd snap her feet together like troops on parade, scatting, "Beat Me Daddy (Eight to The Bar)."

Oh, ladies meeting by chance, who primped each other's hair—netted in a bun, twisted in braids or pinned on top of the head. If one gal's hairdo slipped, another gave a hairpin or bobby, despite the rationing of metal. They were all Betty Grable to me, their snapshots taped to lockers Over There—where the boys all had crewcuts, dreaming in their foxholes of the chesty and the flat, the mousy and the vamps, the freckled and the rouged—as the home front looked in the mirror and made themselves better.

# INHERITANCE

The upstairs furniture went to Charles, the downstairs to Michael. We girls got our parents' wedding crystal, a present from Uncle Max—something small enough to ship to California. Dad sold our Gates Mills home, moved into a dinky apartment with his blue shirts and blue sheets, his lost blue eyes.

Never hold an estate sale while grief is fresh. Mother's wedding dress disappeared. Not that either daughter was petite enough to wear it. Not to mention able to nab a husband. The mother-of-pearl button that clasped my mother's coat sees me now from my button jar amid buttons that never knew her. She was the buttonhole; I was the button. Or the other way around. I wasn't good enough with her and I was no good without her.

# THE GREETING CARD

Even though I knew she was dying, I bought a card that said, *Happy Thanksgiving Day, Mother*. The colors of Rembrandt edged with copper, like the highlights in her hair. Of course, she didn't have her hair anymore.

I kept the card for years. Now and then it surfaced among my souvenirs. What was I supposed to do with it? Finally I gave it to the thrift store and visited it there. It glowed from the rack, unsold. What was wrong with people? What happened to Thanksgiving and Motherhood? Had everyone lost faith, jaded by day-glo colors—Rembrandt wasn't good enough for them anymore? She would have kept the card in her keepsake box with the love letters signed, *Sammy*, the postcards from Uncle Max, and the envelopes with wisps of baby hair. Finally I bought the card.

*To An Insane Degree*

## ANN SEXTON, "RUMPELSTILTSKIN"

*Rumpelstiltskin hears crying through the castle wall. That in itself is extraordinary. Before we even get to the straw-into-gold part. Dwarves always ask for the first-born. And the rich always want more riches. The girl gives him trinkets.*

*He says, "I want some living thing more than all the treasures of the world."*

This is the part people forget—he who mourns no child will ever call him Papa. But even a child knows no one else knew how to spin straw into gold. We *still* don't know. I love Fritz Kredel's illustrations in *Grimms' Fairy Tales*, especially the drawing of Rumpelstiltskin. I love his pointy-toed boots and tall crumpled hat and how the smoke of his campfire reaches up to him like fingers. I hate how the Grimm brothers made Rumpelstiltskin *tear himself asunder*. Why can't he hop by the fire forever, a babe in his arms? In my version, the child is happy to have such a frisky papa, to be warmed by the fire in his blankie of spun gold.

*Sandy Diamond*

# THE EYELESS EARTH

I got a kitten from the shelter, small and gray as a blackboard eraser. I named her Babygirl, which was a stupid mistake. Babygirl perched on my shoulder listless as a shoulder pad. I picked a bouquet of daylilies from the field for her to know there was a great outdoors waiting for her. I played Purcell and Bach while she slept on my chest, weightless as chalk. Her pink nose turned white. How many people know lilies are poisonous to cats? At least she didn't die in a cage, I told myself between sobs.

    Watering the hard summer Grand Ronde ground, thinking of shade, I dug her grave between two incense cedars, forgetting about roots. Why should roots lengthen forever when a kitten is an eyebrow questioning over the eyeless earth? To soften the dirt, I watered the lilac bush. My shovel hit something hard. Naturally, I thought buried treasure, greedy as the next guy. It was the sewer. I was required to be grateful the pipe didn't break. Finally, I thought the peonies would cushion her with their tuberous roots, but it feels like I'll never stop burying her, never stop disinterring in my mind the flowered towel she died in, missing that pretty towel.

# WHEN OHIO WAS TEXAS

When I was eight my, father bought me a Wild West jacket from the Wild West Store.

Mother said, "You're going to have to take it back, or get the other kids one too."

He never did. Fathers don't back down. I rode our collie bareback, her tawny hair and my suede fringe giddyupped like Ohio was Texas, her lean muzzle parting the wind. Through the past-your-bedtime window, the silvery moon shone on me.

Years flew, years I leaned on like a windowsill, like a yearling leans on the leg of its mare. 'Til the day someone left the closet door open and the full-length mirror reined me in. That's when I saw the mirror doesn't care if you have the longest braids and you know all Gene Autry's songs by heart and wail like a coyote so real your parents say, *Please shut up*.

I saw Mother in the mirror behind me. I tried to pull the two halves of the jacket together across my new chest.

"You're blooming," said the same mother I loved as recently as yesterday.

"No I'm not!"

"Look, those shoulders are so tight your arms stick out from your sides. The sleeves end three inches above the wrist. You wear it night and day, it's four years old and filthy and can't be cleaned. The dog is swaybacked from you. Face facts, Hiawatha, today's the day that jacket bites the dust."

*Sandy Diamond*

# MARY

When I was a girl—before anything bad happened—I had a doll with pudgy arms and legs like a real baby, dimpled elbows and inseparable toes. Since Mother worked with Dad at the Tasty Shop, we had a live-in maid named Mary. She sewed dresses for my doll from the fine, flowered burlap bags that chicken seed came in. Maybe it was only one dress because when I picture my doll, I always see the same pattern of tiny flowers. I was so grateful for this dress, I named my doll Mary.

The best thing about Mary was she didn't change. When I held her in my lap, she always gazed right back at me with her round brown eyes. When I laid her down, she'd close her eyes, fall asleep without a fuss, her plump fists where I'd left them.

After my thirteenth birthday, Mother became my stepmother.

"Look at you. You're not a child anymore—"

"Yes, I am—"

"You're too old for dolls—"

"No, I'm not."

But suddenly I wasn't so sure. How did she know this? Was there a book that said so? I was thinking fast to keep up with this new turn of events. One thing I knew was if the new lumps on my chest were a good thing, Michael would have had them. Mother pulled Mary out of my arms.

"Please don't take Mary away."

"We'll just put her here in the closet. See? She'll be nearby."

Mary, sitting on the high shelf in the dark closet, her arms a little raised as if in alarm, as if to hug me, waiting for me to open the door.

How many more years—twenty, thirty?—of staring at children through cyclone fences—other people's children playing in playgrounds, the steel mesh biting my fingers?

## OAKLAND, 1971 MEDICINE MAN

I'd been painting for fifteen years full-time between bouts of madness. Painting was everything. Lying in bed, fragrant with linseed oil and turpentine, looking at the light in the crack of the door, I wanted more. By then, marriage would have fit me like Cinderella's slipper fit Cinderella's sisters.

I went to a Halloween party—not as my usual clown or vamp, but as a wise old woman. I wore the long lace ecru dress Grandmother once wore to weddings, powdered my pinned-up hair. It was there I saw Medicine Man!—feathers, leather, and beads—chanting behind a papier-mâché mask. What a nice package, thought I. He danced with abandon and staying power, the very qualities I sought. All the girls were after him. I was an old lady sitting with decorous knees. Being a genuine medicine man, he saw through my disguise. He saw the life waiting in me. One-quarter Athabaskan, he showed me a matchbook given away by a bank with a picture of an Indian dressed as he was. I loved his honesty. I told him what I wanted. We became lovers that night.

---

Medicine Man was a locksmith. In spring, a gesture spun and tumbled in my womb like a combination lock and we both knew all the numbers. I loved being pregnant. I loved feeling worth giving up your seat on the bus for. It was selfish, I admit—the whole enterprise was selfish—but I refused to live a life of *if only*. At the movies—*McCabe and Mrs. Miller, Last Tango in Paris, The Last Picture Show*—I searched the credits for the most beautiful name: *Gabriel*.

Medicine Man looked like Paul Newman, especially in the dark. This was when my bed was an island of foam on the floor of Valle Vista above the Art Deco Grand Lake Theater with its faux columns and fireworks marquee. After a movie, we'd stroll up Sunny Slope and I'd watch passersby double-take at my Paul Newman look-alike.

## THE HEAVENS AT THE TIME OF YOUR BIRTH

We planned for the baby to be a Libra. This was the early seventies when people believed that how the heavens looked at the time of your birth affected you. It still sounds reasonable to me: Libra for balance. Medicine Man was Aquarius. I, Leo. Before this, I had slept with men whose sign I didn't know.

After a Mexican dinner on the eve of the due date—October fourth, birthday of Buster Keaton and St. Augustine—contractions started at midnight. My housemate Leslie drove me to the hospital in his little Austin-Healey on the empty streets, slower than anyone had ever driven before.

"Faster! Faster! There's no traffic!" I screamed through clenched teeth, clenched everything, my centimeters swiftly dilating.

"I don't want to get into an accident," said Leslie the unrufflable, parking at every stop sign. Three a.m.—so fast there wasn't time for anesthetic—although I yelled for it—so fast instead of *push*, they shouted, *Wait! Hold it!* That baby sailed out of me with a mind of his own. A nurse laid Gabriel on my chest. Gabriel looked at me.

A nurse cried, "He's focused in the delivery room!"

Apgar ten, if you know what that means. It means perfect. Gabriel reached out his newborn hand and patted my cheek. I have witnesses. The doctor handed me scissors: I cut the cord myself. Mijo—my Lamaze coach and French friend—told me later, in France the doctor lets only the most courageous mothers cut the cord, but my doctor said he handed me the scissors so I would remember my child's life was separate from mine. Farid, a Sufi astrologer friend, did Gabriel's natal horoscope. The word *actor* appeared five times.

People said, "Who will share the responsibility?"

I was prepared for the full responsibility. What I wasn't prepared for was sleeping alone, no one to share the joy—no one to see him nursing in the middle of the night, hanging onto my braid in his infant fist, hear him purring like a cat. See the way he'd lift his hand as though holding a baton, and let it fall in an arc, like a conductor orchestrating everything, the flow of milk, the rocking chair, the song I hummed.

*It is night neddying among the snuggeries of babies.*
—*Dylan Thomas*

Dianne moved to Oakland. Maggie and Leslie played hide-and-seek, popping up around his highchair. He laughed and laughed. We were all in the kitchen together when Gabriel said his first word: *allgood*.

"Say it again," we told him, to be sure he knew what he was saying. And he said it again.

We fenced in the yard, created a gate—both ways—in and out. I let you go, dearest thing, and only pretend you are mine. You are yours.

*To An Insane Degree*

# WELCOME TO THE TASTY SHOP

I sent a birth announcement, a vintage drawing of a Native American woman holding a baby in the crook of her arm, the other arm reaching to the sky. A freethinking cousin on Mother's side of the family crocheted an orange tasseled blanket Gabriel slept under until his feet stuck out the bottom. Some relatives were scandalized.

Daddy wrote, "Don't send any more announcements."

I flew my son to Cleveland—the Tasty Shop—for everyone to see. Past the cigarette machine, the cash register, deli counter, soda fountain, the leatherette booths where the waitresses sat on their break between lunch and dinner. My old comrades I hadn't seen for three years. We beamed at each other; they started to get up when I saw they saw the bundle in my arms. They peered behind me for Mr. D who wasn't there. That's when I realized he hadn't told them. Later he told me he couldn't bring himself to say, "My daughter had a baby out of wedlock. I am the caterer of my synagogue—what did you expect me to tell the help?"

I inched closer to Gladys, Charlotte, and Marge, and the others—my old pals. They craned their necks to see what was inside the blanket.

I said, "This is my son, Gabriel." To my dismay, this came out in a squeak instead of the joyous scene I had imagined. For years, we had worked and joked together. The oldest ones knew me as a child. One of Marge's favorite expressions was, "Don't that beat all?" I saw Gabriel seeing them—eight women dressed all alike in light-green uniforms trimmed in white, caps held in place with bobby pins. Apron pockets heavy with well-deserved tips, their big hearts heavy with their own heartaches. I could see them at Mother's funeral and knew I might not have had the courage to have this child while she was alive. I knew they were thinking, "What would Mrs. D have thought?"

They peered at Gabriel. He peered back.

"Coo coo," Marge said.

"He's beautiful."

"Are you coming home?"

"California is my home now. I went there to have this baby."

I wanted them to see how happy I was—they who knew who I used to be in the breakdown years. But seeing them, what I really wanted was for Mother to see, touch, embrace him.

"Welcome to the Tasty Shop," I whispered to my baby.

---

Mother left me enough for a down payment on a classic Berkeley brown shingle on Derby Street just above College. Four bedrooms, an attic, guestroom—room for Maggie, Leslie, Farid, and Ted—baker of pies. No matter what you said to him he said, "Is that right?" And Victor Malafronte, frisbee champion. Ethereal Blackbird and Ponderosa Pine—all were Gabriel's teachers. Their motto: be useful, love beauty, adapt. When a plague killed blackbirds in the area, Blackbird changed her name to Laughingbird.

I thought loving this child would outsmart manic depression. But I was wrong. I'd drop Gabriel off at preschool, nursery school, kindergarten, and go to the park to sleep, hidden by shrubbery away from any path. Then wake up in time to get Gabriel, and pretend nothing was wrong.

Three years old, Gabriel in his car seat at a red light. A man crossed the street in front of us, eating an orange and dropping the peel. Gabriel looks at me. He knew about littering.

"He must be very sad," he said.

I usually shopped at Value Village, but for my birthday, my sister gave me a poncho from Macy's. The colors were too bold for me—I went with Gabriel to exchange it for something more subtle. Four years old, the first time he had seen such a large and luxurious store. When I pulled a poncho over my head, I lost sight of him. I called his name softly, then more loudly, searching the displays, until slowly a circular rack of long-sleeved silk blouses slowly revolving without any visible means of locomotion caught my eye.

"Gabriel?" I asked, peering into the pastel carousel. Lying on his back, feet in silk, he pedaled the spokes of the rack, the long sleeves caressing his face.

My father sent money for a washing machine—one hundred dollars, so I wouldn't have to go to the laundromat with my bad back. Suddenly euphoric, I spent it all at a vintage bookstore on Solano Avenue, for the beauty of the fine old bindings, the gilded lettering, and illustrations on the spines.

# LUCK

Gabriel slept in an antique bed in a sleeping porch off my bedroom. An orange kite with a rainbow and stars, a circus mobile, a lace curtain, and a Bonnard still life print. Outside, an old tree embraced the second story room windows. I pulled up a little chair to his bed to read him bedtime stories, leaning over to show him the pictures.

A boy in an orange shirt and yellow pants floats from a parachute on the cover of *What Good Luck! What Bad Luck!* by Remy Charlip. The boy is invited to a surprise party—what good luck! He imagines food, presents, a cake. But turning the page, we learn the party is in Florida and the boy is in New York. What bad luck! But on the next page, someone loans him an airplane. Good luck! He's wearing an aviator's cap and goggles, his long scarf blowing in the wind, flying over tall buildings! What good luck! But on the next page, the motor explodes! Bad luck! Turn the page—the parachute! But there's a hole in the parachute. Now the boy is tiny, falling headfirst through space. But wait—good luck—there's a haystack on the ground. But oh no—there's a pitchfork in the haystack! We're at the mercy of looming disaster or gleeful delivery at each turn. I read this book to Gabriel every night for three years and then he read it to me, both of us yelling, *Good luck! Bad luck!*

# THE GUILLOTINE

For my son's fourth birthday party, I hired a magician named Happy the Clown. He appeared at our Berkeley home in tie-dyed OshKosh B'gosh overalls and a magic guillotine. When he showed the instrument of death to the nine tie-dyed birthday guests, they screamed with joy. But when Happy asked for a volunteer to put his finger in the machine, the room fell silent.

"Let me show you—it's harmless," he said and stuck a carrot with its head of greens in the little guillotine and dropped the blade. Half the carrot hit the floor. Happy examined the beheaded vegetable, shaking its green head at the boys.

"Oh well," he said, "Let's try again with a real finger!"

All the once bloodthirsty four-year-olds suddenly sat on their hands.

"Hey, Rainbow, Black Panther, Unicorn—who will lay his finger on the line?"

"What a bunch of establishment flunkies! Okay, suckers, I get paid to do this—how 'bout a mother?"

Suddenly, the mothers were in the kitchen, cooking weenies.

The boys were silent to a man. Up stood my friend Madelaine, who always looked ethereal. She sidled up to the wizard and his ambiguous contraption.

"Finger, please," said Happy. "Anyone you want." ("I mean any one you *don't* want.")

"Don't do it!" the children screamed, looking for their moms.

The executioner turned to me. "Just to be on the safe side, a bowl from the kitchen, if you please."

A groan rose from the guests large and small. I fetched a bowl I didn't like, knelt, and tried to steady it under Maddy's trembling hand, which was white as Wite-Out. Meanwhile I'm racking my brain for who recommended this clown. Woosh falls the blade, and Madelaine, blood rushing back to her face, waves all ten fingers in the metaphysical Berkeley air.

## WALL STREET

Right out of college, 1961, I had a gig on Wall Street. From Schraft's downtown, I'd wheel my cart of croissants, crumpets, and Danishes up the cobblestone street to the Stock Exchange. In the basement, the mailroom boys got first pick, slipping change slow-motion deep into my frilly apron pocket. Someone always tried to pinch my buns. Up each floor, the air conditioning smelling like money, the carpeting thick as thieves. At the top floor, men howled into a telephone jungle, gesturing for jelly or glazed. Once, a guy tipped me five bucks for snagging him the last Napoleon.

Once, a joker pulled the strings of my prim Schrafty apron—my hands full of puffs and steam, puffs and steam.

# EARTHQUAKE

Geologists and psychics alike were predicting The Big One. A scientist on one area's newspaper's Lost Pets column: A record number of cats and dogs were missing. Four feet on the ground, they knew things we didn't. I started wrapping things up. The family photographs huddled together on the floor like evacuees. Grandmother's cut crystal bowl and all the blue-and-white china were ghosts in towels.

"What am I supposed to dry with?" Gabriel, six, yelled from the shower. "What am I supposed to eat off of?" he hollered from the kitchen. "I thought we were *against* paper plates!" In the morning, he surveyed his room (which was always in upheaval) and asked, "Did the earthquake come?"

# THE RED SHOES

Rilke was a manic-depressive. Someone he knew also knew Freud and urged the poet to see the psychiatrist.

Rilke famously said, "Your doctor may take away my devils but ah, what of my angels?"

This quote had been my battle cry. My losses were legion. Gabriel changed the equation—to have him was to give up the option of bowing out. Gabriel made me live just as once painting did—there was no backing down. Having Gabriel, I'd trapped myself into life.

Feeling the approach of Hyde's despair, I went to Dr. X. She was strong and glamorous. She looked like the models in *Vogue* I'd been leafing through in the waiting room, turning the pages roughly, past each unattainable beauty. Trotting out my sad story to Dr. X, I thought: she cannot know my life.

"Have you painted lately?" she asked.

I realized it had been years since I'd done any art apart from sketching my housemates and Gabriel. To take meds was to betray Rilke, selling out to chemistry.

"But what are you selling?" Dr. X asked and answered, "You are selling despair. And have you found any buyers?"

She said one word: "Lithium."

Dr. X told me Robert Lowell had gotten lithium in 1967. I was furious I had fought this fight for ten unnecessary years, holding onto a thread of sanity. She said sixty percent of her patients were successful. Lithium was like California: the end of the line. If you couldn't find happiness in California, then you might as well jump in the sea.

I wept, "Help me take off the red shoes."

Every morning I took a small pink capsule that would save or further ruin my life. I stared in the mirror, looking for change—Hyde back to Jekyll.

"Is this the day I'll be a normal person?" I wondered. *Change me*, I said to the pill, to the mirror.

Lithium is a soft lustrous element, the lightest known metal. It floats on water. It imparts a crimson color to a flame. The old ecstasy and despair still hover like a lit match, but they have ceased committing arson and grand larceny of the soul.

I asked my doctor if her other patients felt or acted as I did. I needed to know if there were others like me or if I was the only one. Where was I on a scale of one to ten? Just to know where I stood on the scaffold of mental health.

"I don't take polls," she said.

"Just give me a signal. Let's say I'm going to tell you something special—cross your legs if it's common—wink if you've never heard it before."

Shrinks expect you to tell all—they all went to sphinx school. I had an exhibit. Dr. X came. She bought my most recent oil—a yellow flowered ashtray hovering above paint-splattered space—at the bottom a coiled umber seashell. She had it framed in the thin white metal I like, so the image seems to float out of itself, hover on to the surrounding space. She hung it on her office wall where a seashell wound-up in itself and a flowered ashtray brimmed over. She saw me at one with my art. Sometimes when we spoke, I'd see her looking beyond me to the painting. She knew it was me—the part of me that was leaving the craziness behind. As for sexual desire diminishing, I had been so prone to love and lovemaking that the portion lithium took away just brought me down to the national average.

# BARTLEBY

I started seeing things I hadn't seen before, things that must have been there all along. My eyes landed on a flyer on a telephone pole on Grove Street—which had just changed its name to Martin Luther King Jr. Way, Milky Way. I noticed the swoopy lowercase "g" advertising a class in astrology. Then, tacked on a vermilion door, a haiku written in brush. I wanted to make letters like that. When I had to learn to walk again after the fracture, I was a baby taking baby steps. Learning to make beautiful letters—*Humanist Bookhand, Black Letter, Legend*—was like that. Walking and writing the second time around was harder. And more precious.

*Mythology tells us that where you stumble, that's where your treasure is.*—Joseph Campbell

I joined San Francisco's Friends of Calligraphy. Workshops with geniuses of lettering. I missed painting, but there was a kinship between oil painting and writing with a brush and thick sumi ink. The mark was the same—sensuous, fluid, and free. I started with the fifteenth-century *Rotunda*. Put caps on those letters and they're Tweedledee and Tweedledum. You pack them up against each other. A line of Uncial links hands like chain mail, a fat little army, chanting, *the pen is mightier than the sword*. Yet Uncial is the hand of prayer. How I wanted to be an early monk or nun in a scriptorium, copying and illuminating the gospels. Uncial was the last all-uppercase hand, before ascenders and descenders punctured the space. Before then, everything was contained between two lines—safe and round as donuts.

We perched on high stools like Bartleby the Scrivener. Nothing for the spine's ache to lean against. Unshapely, I willed losing the body's wayward curve in the shapeliness of alphabets:

*a a a a a* 'til the end of the row. *b b b b b*, circling the best one.

My favorite letter was the voluptuous lowercase g—the only letter you can take wild liberties without losing legibility.

*"The great, grey-green, greasy Limpopo*
*River/All set about with fever trees."*

—Rudyard Kipling

# AMPERSANDS OF LOVE

I became enamored of the double-jointed ampersand, between Y and Z—the twenty-seventh character that they don't teach you in school. So many ways to make it, always an arm swooping up to hold out a flat palm as though to say, *I'm giving you all I have. But hey, there's more after that.*

Oh, if I could find a lad as lasting as an ampersand.

Or was my ampersand Eli, the Shakespearean scholar who cradled his mandolin like a mother & her child played bluegrass & one night we rolled from his mattress over tattered rugs ecstatic, not stopping until we hit the bookcase of *Sonnets & Comedies*. Quiet Eli & his drift of blond hair falling over his brow—yes, like Orlovsky's hair fell over his blessed brow & it was Eli, one of those 113th Street years, who hitched to Gates Mills during his finals to woo me from woe. That year—one of those years—I was trying to leave the world, praying to Peter Pan, *come for me, take me*—God, you keep doing this—I'm not going to put up with it much longer, send me a lad who'll stay longer than a mood swing.

*1958 & everyone was sleeping with everyone else except me & the air, fragrant as mangos, a neon sign flashing off & on: This is how to lose your mind. &* Howie jumped into my bed & out again fast when it dawned on him I didn't know how to make love but froze & had to be told to put my arms around him instead of lying there passive as flypaper, & he cried, *I'm not sleeping with no fucking virgin!,* informing me virgins always fall in love with their first lover & stick around, then you can't get rid of them.

## WHAT GOD WANTS OF US

In *The Story of Writing*, Donald Jackson—scribe to the Queen of England—illustrates a tiny self-portrait of the twelfth-century scribe Adelhard The Nun. I keep thinking her name is *Addlehard*. What if—even with calligraphy, even with the protection of the church—she sometimes couldn't think straight? Perhaps the devil jostled her hand and there was no way to correct a mistake. No, even if you accidentally wrote something twice or left out a whole page, you had to keep going. So, these texts come down to us with glaring or incomprehensible errors in the holy words. How then can we know what God wants of us?

## QUICKSILVER PINIONS & PERMANENCE

My favorite calligraphy teacher was the master of *Brush Script*, San Francisco's Alan Blackman. His motto was, *the brush is mightier than the pen.* Instead of the same letter over and over again, he assigned us goofy sentences containing every letter of the alphabet to be written with Designer's Gouache in zero- and thirty-degree pen angles and in both three and four pen widths:

*Cruising with poets & mystics, few visits to Xanadu & Zanzibar were more joke than quest.*

*Two hardy boxing kangaroos jet from Sydney to Zanzibar on quicksilver pinions.*

Or single letter exercises:

*The crabby cabbie dragged the bedraggled cabbage to the garbage.*

If you didn't learn how to make *g*'s after that, you never would.

---

Alan taught his students what was permanent and what was not. We painted a sample of all the colors of gouache we used. Then we masked off the lower half of the color row and taped the page to a window. After a month, when we removed the tape, the permanent colors were as we painted them; the portion of the fugitive colors that had been exposed to sunlight appeared in faded contrast to the part concealed. We saw with our own eyes that Ultramarine is as intense unmasked as it was before, and my darling Bistre went from sepia to a ghost of itself.

*Sandy Diamond*

# MONASTERY & SERIFS

I begged Alan to let me be his apprentice—clean his brushes, feed his rabbit, drive him anywhere. At last, he let me escort him to the Carmelite monastery in San Rafael, where the nuns were making a calligraphic presentation to a visiting bishop. Between us and the sisters was a metal grill through which—without a word—they passed their scrolled homework. Alan smoothed out the roll, showed me the alarmingly primitive writing, and passed it back with praise. Slowly, I understood they were not writing to be scribes; they were writing to serve the word of God. Alan told me God didn't care if the slant was consistent and each bowl was harmonious with the ones before.

Lunch was provided to us via a dumbwaiter. We carried our simple tasty fare to the lawn, sitting in the tasseled grass. Although I was full of questions, the nuns' vow of silence was contagious. Alan said communication happened through the hymns they copied out in *Italic* or *Humanist Bookhand*. Before returning the trays to the dumbwaiter, Alan plucked a handful of grass and spelled out THANK YOU in *Roman Caps*, pinching the tassels into serifs. Hoist and fall, the dumbwaiter of my heart—not mood swings—but a way to convey my love for this new life.

---

When I was young, learning to read, I put my fingers in the holes—oh black and shiny telephone!—to touch all the letters. Recessed, because they were precious. That's how new life used to be. I'd pick up the receiver, hold its tiny holes to my ear, and however fast I did it, a living operator was always there saying, *"To whom may I connect you?"*

The great English scribe Edward Johnson hung a poster of the holy Roman Capitals from the Trajan column, written around the year 113, in his outhouse. He liked to absorb, while there, how a serif enters a letter as though he were the middleman in the circle of life. A scribe who had visited Johnson's privy told us you couldn't sit there without shitting serifs. My understanding was serifs were invented when the Roman stonecutters tried to carve the main column of an I, for instance. Hitting the chisel directly into the body of the letter might shatter the stone. Easing the chisel in a shallow, small distance from the desired cut gave birth to the elegance of the Roman alphabet. Before I learned this, I made the letter and then stuck on the serifs. My letters looked like they were wearing graduation hats. Slowly, slowly, I learned to treat serifs like a caress entering the body of the letter so that serif and main stroke were one.

One of my teachers told this story:

*In China, long ago, a cook planned to open a seafood restaurant. He paid an artist to paint a fish for the business signs. Weeks passed, and the cook waited patiently, dreaming of fish, both painted and cooked. After a month, the cook visited the painter's shop. His eyes darted like minnows around the studio: no fish.*

*"My shop is opening next week," said the cook. "Where is my fish?"*

*"Not ready yet," said the artist.*

*The cook visited the artist every day, hoping to catch sight of his fish. The restaurant opened. No one came. People didn't know it was there. Wringing his hands, the cook said, "It doesn't have to be the best fish in the world. I'll take any fish. Just give me something, I beg of you."*

*The artist took up a signboard, paints, and brushes and in a few quick strokes created the most beautiful fish the cook had ever seen.*

*Embracing the artist, the cook exclaimed, "Thank you, Master, but if you could do this, why didn't you do it months ago?"*

*The artist opened a closet door—a thousand painted fish swam into the room.*

*Sandy Diamond*

# CHANCE

Years later—1971—when I was running out of baby-making years, Chance, a cowboy too young to be a daddy but not too young for the first deliberate single mother in the universe (as I liked to think of myself) jammed with Sonny Terry and Brownie McGhee in the downtown clubs. And bad luck—he was the perfect age to be drafted and when he had to disappear even though he went to all those Friends meetings. He sent me a long-handled carved maple spoon, nestled in Vermont's autumn leaves, and wrote wistful letters in green ink in up-slanting lines like newly planted crops. Green ink like my New York drawings of Robbie and Eli long ago. He who first felt my baby's new life turn.

Photo: me in a purple hippie dress, Chance in a straw Stetson, his cowboy hand on my new belly. And once I knew I was safely pregnant from Medicine Man and thus could finally sleep with Chance—slim Chance, last chance—we did. Madness had robbed me of love in my twenties—why shouldn't I have that love now? That old bargain with God? Statute of limitations, baby. Here we are on Mt. Diablo, Chance balancing Gabriel laughing into the sky—the infinite azure cerulean ultramarine sky. After one of the sweetest friendships of my life, Chance left to try his chances north. I wanted to stay where I was.

## EINSTEIN & GERTRUDE STEIN

To earn a living, I started with certificates. I loved writing names—each one a different way to design the same space. The names of Gabriel's graduating classes in Gothic Cursive. Seeing the letters of children's names flow from my pen—for the children to see themselves, a new form made visible.

Juried street fairs: people lined the booth reading Einstein, Gertrude Stein, Groucho Marx, Dickinson, and Little Richard. Crafts fairs in Berkeley, Oakland, Sausalito, Palo Alto. Made prints of the best-selling originals so more people could afford them. One year at the San Francisco Women's Holiday Fair, Alice Walker bought a quote someone had seen on a t-shirt:

*There is nothing*
*nothing*
*nothing*
*two women*
*cannot do*
*before noon*

"I'm giving it to Gloria Steinem," she said.

Now I could say my work was in the Gloria Steinem Collection.

The following year, I had calligraphed a quote from Moms Mabley:
*Don't tell me 'bout the good old days—I was there—where was they?*

Whoopi Goldberg was the entertainment at the Women's Building, trying out the act that would next year make her famous. She passed by my booth in her Black skintight kickass dreadlocked adorableness.

"Whoopi, look—Moms!" I cried, holding the quote up above the crowd.

She stopped, read it, reached for it, and gave me two tickets to Moms' show. Now my work was in The Whoopi Goldberg Collection.

The next ten years I taught calligraphy with drawing, painting, or collage. Lithium gave me the courage to learn something new. Calligraphy healed me.

# GRAPHOLOGY

One year at Stanford University's spring fair, the sign of the booth next to mine read: *Who You Are: five dollars. Who You Can Be: ten.* Students lined up to write the sentence devised to reveal their secret selves.

Eavesdropping, I heard, "Margins, pressure, space between lines, between words, between letters. Rhythm. Size. Slant. Departure from a straight line."

The graphologist Robert Wasserman admonished one person for tangling his ascenders and descenders—"There madness lies. But don't worry, Beethoven did it too"—and praised someone else for lassoing her t's: persistence. To a scoffer, he claimed, "The science of handwriting was good enough for Aristotle, Shakespeare, and Emerson." I loved this guy. I wanted to know everything he knew. Thus began my correspondence course in graphology.

"What is handwriting," Erasmus said, "but silent speech?"

If I weren't already obsessed with calligraphy, I'd have thrown myself into this luscious discipline, get licensed, analyze signatures, expose forgers in court, defend the rightful heirs. But I'm just a dilettante, amusing friends at parties. Remember in *Dr. Jekyll and Mr. Hyde*, how the doctor's friends first suspected Jekyll and Hyde were the same person? The only thing that resists disguise is their handwriting! To change his hand, Hyde sloped his script backward. Even so, a student of handwriting saw the damning resemblance.

We can look at a page of handwriting as landscape. We draw ourselves into the world. Or shy away from it. The right margin: do we plan ahead or stop when there is enough space to go on? Handwriting is self-portrait and we can't fake it. Looking at a letter from Herb Weiss, 1961, when I was faltering in New York—two pages of his round, looped cursive and every *t* lassoed. I knew he never would have given up on me. Or anyone.

Sandy Diamond

# HOW TO DRAW A LION

I had this crazy idea that if I could do something courageous, Gabriel—then seven—would see me as strong and brave and overlook my weakening body. I took my sketchbook to the lions' cage at the Oakland Zoo. Where the visitors stand, you can't get close enough to see the details. I found the zookeeper.

"Zookeeper, may I go behind the cages where you feed the animals and draw the lion from there?"

"Against the rules," he said.

"Just for twenty minutes?" I begged, showing him my sketchbook from the San Francisco Aquarium: a tortoise riding on an alligator's tail. I could see he liked the drawing or maybe just liked the animals or liked seeing one animal on top of another.

"Twenty minutes," he said. "You don't have to tell anyone else about this."

"Never," I swore. Of course, I planned to tell Gabriel, but the zookeeper would never know. With an enormous ring of keys, he unlocked a metal door behind the cages. Along a narrow hallway, live exhibits stirred, pungent with dung the size of Stonehenge. A tiger, then two bears and a cub turned to see where this new smell—me—was coming from. When were they last fed? I might have wondered sooner.

Suddenly, the lion. Me still as a grave marker, back pressed against the wall. Six feet from his bars.

"Don't get him riled up," the zookeeper said, and I knew I'd made a mistake.

"Don't talk to him. He doesn't know your voice. If he's looking at you—and he will—his back's to the public. They won't like that," he said, trudging down the fuggy hall.

First the eyes. Then the triangular mouth and the broad feline nose. I drew a jagged line from forehead to cheekbone. The mane electrified. I felt him in my pen, my fingers, and arm. I had him. Was it the motion of paper as I turned the page? Suddenly he unfolded, stood and roared, thrashing his tufted tail. The sound was nothing like the MGM lion. It was like high C to crystal. I was going to die alone in the stench. But my child would take the drawing to school, unscroll it in front of the class, and say, "This is the lion that ate my mom."

"Help!" I cried to the crowd beyond the lion's cage, in a bad dream's puny squeak, afraid to wave my arms.

People were looking around for where the human voice was coming from. "Zookeeper, find the zookeeper!" I cried. "Look! I'm here! Behind the lion! Save me!"

When after forty minutes the zookeeper and his blessed keys finally unlocked the cage, he had a sheepish expression.

"A parrot in trouble," he mumbled.

As for my son, he was disappointed.

"I'm not taking your stupid drawing to school if the lion didn't eat you," he said.

*Sandy Diamond*

# EDGAR ALLAN POE

When he was eight, Gabriel had a grade school assignment to embody an author the class had been reading. He dressed like the illustration on our deck of *Authors* playing cards—Edgar Allen Poe in a black cape, spooky smudges under his eyes, and a stringy bow tie. He recited from *The Raven* in a melancholy voice:

*What this grim, ungainly, ghastly, gaunt and ominous bird of yore*
*Meant in croaking "Nevermore."*

He was ten. Watching him from the cloakroom, I saw he wasn't Gabriel anymore. He was Poe.

## WHAT IS GREEN?

Our friend Ira asked us this riddle:
*What is green, hangs on the wall, and whistles?*
When we gave up, he said, "A fish."
"A fish isn't green," said Gabriel.
"You could paint it green."
"A fish doesn't hang on the wall!"
"You could hang it on the wall."
"Well,"—thinking we got him this time—we yelled, "A fish doesn't whistle!"
"So…" he said with a resigned shrug and Yiddish accent, "it doesn't vistle."

Sandy Diamond

# THE ZODIAC STREETS

*they say goldfish have no memory*
*I guess their lives are much like mine*
*and the little plastic castle*
*is a surprise every time*

—Ani DiFranco

The convenience store across from us at Parker and McGee got robbed. When we heard gunfire in the night, we knew it was time to move. I fell in love with a 1940s bungalow in the Oakland Hills. Not way up where you had to be rich, but halfway up, between Broadway and the zodiac streets. A Quick Stop across the street, two blocks from the Highway 24 overpass for a fast getaway.

"Just close your eyes," the realtor said. "You'd be surprised how soon the freeway sounds like the ocean."

Coved ceilings, archways instead of doors. To not have to open an interior door meant there was no point at which you could say: this space begins here, ends here. The blessed architect made that space flow, offering a sense of drifting without obstacles. No doorknobs. There was an underground room with its own entrance for Gabriel.

Impractical, if you wanted a private bedroom. I found a folding screen at the Alameda Flea Market, painted it. For the first time from bed, I watched the crescent moon in the living room window teasing each pane, its horns seduced by the winking glass.

Morning: I woke to a glaring light falling on the Chinese rug by my bed—a soft rose and blue. Superimposed on it I saw the hospital rug Michael Dreyfuss had described to me long ago. And it came to me that the 1965 rug was imaginary. Michael had made it up, making me forget for a few moments that I was broken, making believe something beautiful could be near me, just out of sight.

"I am remembering! I am remembering!" I cried.

Gabriel came running up the stairs, asked, "What's your problem?"

# GUNS-R-US

Gabriel was fifteen. He wanted a gun. After years of archery in Tilden Park, he was gifted in timing, aim, control. He promised he'd go to the firing range and observe all the safety precautions. He wouldn't tell his friends. He'd do anything if I'd just take him to the gun store and pretend the gun was for me.

There were a million Saturday night specials in glass cases at Guns-R-Us. Rifles hung from the ceiling, little pearl-handled pistols for the ladies. Gabriel zeroed in on a .22 Luger pistol. Blasé, he corrected the salesman about the safety lock. I was under the sway of his sudden expertise, his focus, and his desire. He'd saved up the money.

When we returned to the store after the waiting period, the salesman was all smiles. Another gun on the street—just what Oakland needed. Now that Gabriel had what he wanted, I started bargaining for the scraps. A lock for his door, which he must pay for. An oath he must sign, swearing he won't tell anyone about the gun. Take the marksmanship course every Saturday morning until he earned a certificate.

The firing range was up a mountain, a long harrowing switchback road with no guard rails. The range was peaceful in comparison. Despite everything—the noise, no place to sit where I could see him, the fact that he was the only child among men—I was surprised by the rush of pride I felt for him, his concentration. So many bull's-eyes. He was a born shooter.

One day, I came home to find the lock broken, the gun gone.

"Why would anyone break into your room? Why would anyone think you had a gun?"

"Someone must have found out," Gabriel said.

The gun, the gun in my mind, the gun in my name. Years later, my son told me he faked the break-in and sold the gun. He was tired of it. He wanted the money. "You are so easy to fool," he said.

# GULLIBLE

One day, when I was calligraphing Kit Carson's dying words *Wish I had time for one more bowl of chili* Gabriel and his friends Elliott and Joaquin clattered up the stairs into my study.

"Mom," Gabriel said, "We were looking up the word gullible and it isn't in the dictionary!"

"Of course, it is. You're probably spelling it wrong."

"No, we really looked."

"It has two *ll*'s."

"Mom, it isn't there."

"It has an *i*, not an *a*."

"Mom, we're telling you!"

"Bring me the dictionary." My *Oxford Universal Dictionary*, four inches thick. Gabriel thumped the tome on my table. As I opened it to the G's, the three boys clattered back downstairs, laughing their heads off.

*Sandy Diamond*

# THE TALKING HEADS

"Listen to the music, listen to this part. Stop what you're doing. Look up from there, you're always writing. Listen to this part right here. Did you hear it? I'll play it again. I can tell you didn't hear it. This time, listen."

When Gabriel dances to the music, his body comes apart like the ocean, like clouds all floaty. He moves unanatomically—legs, hips here then there, head bopping, mouth p pop popping the music inside of him, teeth chompin' on the chompas, hair all bangs and pompadours—

"If I slick it back, I'll look just like David Byrne."

His favorite cap's his Santa hat. He's always losing the bell. The Salvation Army gives him a new bell.

"Listen to this, it sounds tinny. Hear that high pitch? I want my first bell back. The bell was the best part. And it's so cold out there. Get me a wool sweater, will you? Not the woofa woofa wool but the hoppa hoppa wool."

He dances like a boy in the right kind of sweater—he leaps, he twirls, he indicates that he is warm.

"Watch this!" he says. "I may hit the ceiling this time. How close was I? Were you watching?"

The mirror shivers and warps. Over the years, it's gotten slow. He's got the jump on it, appearing in the glass seconds after he's made his move. The mirror gives everything back, not just the dance but the music, the song—

## TELL IT TO THE MARINES

When I was congratulating myself for being a deliberate single mother, I didn't think about my child's teenage rebellion—that there'd be no one to rebel against but me. He must have been fifteen or sixteen, angry at me for trying to keep him from leaving the house in the middle of the night to meet someone under the freeway overpass. To buy what? Yelling at each other, cursing, making threats. Towering over me, he was taller than yesterday, oh precious yesterday. I picked up the phone and fake-dialed the sheriff.

"Sheriff's department? I need help!" I said. "Please send someone over right away. My son…" This phony confession sent me into strangled sobs. Gabriel was the dearest thing in the world to me and I was ratting on him to the authorities. The seventies died that night. Whether I'm a lousy actor or because he heard the dial tone, Gabriel laughed and laughed.

"Call the sheriff!" he said. "Call the Marines! They'll come and arrest you for being an ugly old hag!"

Later, it occurred to me that Oakland didn't have a sheriff.

*Sandy Diamond*

# LETTERS FELL FROM HIS SLEEVE

My father flew out to see Gabriel graduate from high school, resplendent and suddenly mature in his red gown. I hung my calligraphy for Dad to see and invited friends.

He sat just inside the front door, saying to visitors, "Come right in," as though it was the Tasty Shop. "I'm the artist's father," he said. He said that all day long. We reminisced about when I was a child, watching letters fall from his sleeve.

Two days before he died, Daddy beat his thumb on the metal side of the hospital bed as he used to on the breakfast room table, correcting our manners.

"What's the song, Dad?"

"*Waltz*," he said, taking his time, "*of The Flowers.*"

Dianne and I hummed Tchaikovsky, amazed we knew it. Songs from family trips, Ohio scrolling by. At *Down by The Old Mill Stream* he joined in, his dying voice another kind of music. The nurses paused in the doorway—they didn't know he had it in him.

Two days before he died, when we thought he was sleeping, and we were putting together an order of take-out from the nearby deli, he opened his famous blue eyes and said, "I'll have a corned beef combo."

How we laughed and reached to touch him. On the day before he died, when all four of his children were by his bed watching him sleep, he suddenly said, "Let's get crackin," making us jump one last time.

A voice from behind the flimsy curtain, separating Dad from an invisible neighbor, said, "Is that Sam Diamond over there? He used to be a big shot."

Furious, I hissed to the curtain, "Shut up! Shut up! We don't want to hear another peep out of you!"

Later, when I told Dianne, she said she would have said, "He's *still* a big shot!"

On the last day, his face was smooth as a stone—his Daddy face without a line in it, suddenly yellow as the moon. If there is a heaven—and there better be—he's a big shot there, eternally.

After the funeral, Dianne and I fly back to the West Coast, the clouds glowed like the locomotive smoke of Monet's *La Gare Saint-Lazare*. Who will I tell that to now? A pool of light glowed like the satin pillow beneath my father's head in his rosewood coffin.

# HAIGHT STREET

So I was on Haight Street today, James—my Offenbach singer friend. I didn't mean to look for you. The shops are impossible now, my dear—not what you knew. I thought I glimpsed the veiled hat, blond wig—your own hair disappearing by then—you wore to that last party, when a flowered teacup trembled in my lap.

Haight Street is flimsier without you, less witty. Where is your butler's *hauteur* that might have kept the standards up? William said you went so fast, with all your grace intact. You are considered among the lucky ones. This is what luck has come down to.

On the last day, you said, "I wish I could walk down Haight Street once more."

But I think if there is any justice in the world, you left in time, before the plague was commonplace. This is what justice has come down to.

# MYSTIFYING PATHS

Circling the mystifying paths of Golden Gate Park, looking for a shady grove. There's supposed to be a sign.

"Don't expect a flower garden," we'd been warned.

Oh, easy to find Shakespeare's Garden, his darling buds of May. Someone told me when you read the dates on the markers, you cry, "1983! But he was just twenty!"

Then you see they were all in their twenties. Or thirties. Forty's rare. Mica, James, do you like the quiet setting the city's Parks and Rec made for you? Or would you have preferred vermillion gladiolas, purple orchids, birds of paradise?

Somewhere where I can't find you, you sleep in woolly thyme, fragrant elfin thyme, nettle's heart-shaped leaves, slender leaves on slender stems.

*Sandy Diamond*

# HITLER'S SOCKS

I was rifling through the Land's End sale catalog when Men's Accessories came into view. As if my son let me shop for him. As if he wore ties. I used to buy my dad neckties—paisley in blue or maroon. No sweetheart to give flannel boxers to or an aviator belt. Skip that page. But the next page reads "Hitler's Socks." Blood rushes to my face as at a stamp collectors' show once, when next to stamps of Beethoven and Bach, a sudden page of swastikas. At second glance, the catalogue said "Hiker's Socks," Olive or Khaki. Fully padded, they absorb shocks as Hitler's army hikes across Czechoslovakia, Poland, Land's End. Nazi feet trample my grandparents' neighbors who didn't get out when the getting was good. I'm not ordering Hitler socks, damn the savings.

# GERTRUDE & ALICE & SAMMY

Telegraph Avenue, Berkeley, the bookstore window of Shakespeare & Co. The title *Dear Sammy* caught my eye. *Sammy* was how my father signed his love letters to Mother. The book was subtitled *Letters from Gertrude Stein and Alice B. Toklas, Edited with a Memoir by Samuel M. Steward*. Marked down to two dollars. That's how I learned Samuel Steward was living in Berkeley. I was working on a collection of quotes about risk and passion. I wrote to him for permission to use excerpts from his memoir. His response was elegant, kind, and on good paper.

He invited me to his cottage on Tenth Street. In his garden was a scrawny rosebush named *Blush Noisette* from the garden of the chateau near Culoz. A rose from Gertrude Stein is of course a rose quite apart from any other rose. I wish I could say it was flourishing. It must be hard to adapt from the French Republic to the People's Republic of Berkeley. Over the course of several visits, there was nowhere to sit in his tiny living room but under Steward's huge male nude sculpture, looking at it no more than necessary. Nor at the explicit illustrations displayed from his pornographic books written under the name *Phil Andros*—what I called his *nom de penis*. I soaked up Sam's stories of being gay on two continents in the thirties and forties. How, through their lovers, he connected with Whitman (a pat on the head from an intimate whom the poet had patted on the head) and Wilde—a romp in Lord Alfred Douglas's bed. He showed me a filmy silk scarf Gertrude had given him. Then, with both hands he held before me—as though I might try to snatch it away—her handwritten birthday poem to him I'd seen photographed in books. Her actual writing. On the paper she wrote on.

Her script slanted up the page at a pronounced forward angle—high ascenders, deep descenders, inflated capitals. The repeated *y*'s of *birthday* and *Sammy* created a rhythm of diagonal slashes. No superfluous strokes, the sign of a brilliant mind racing. What most sets her hand apart is the great distance between the lines, as though she were casting her thoughts into borderless space. Which is what she did.

Sam had visited Gertrude and Alice in France when war permitted. In his memoir he tells this story: Hitler was advancing on Paris where Stein and Toklas, both Jews, had that famous collection of art. Steward asked if they had a plan:

*"Never mind about us,"* Gertrude said, *"we'll be alright. The peasants will hide us if necessary. It may be dangerous, but we have almost decided that's what we're going to do.*

"But the pictures in Paris!" I said. "The Germans will take them all!"

*Even in the dark, I could see her wink.*

*"We are going back there secretly if war comes and bundle some of them up and bring them here."*

"O my god," I said. "If Paris falls and the Germans find you, they'll kill you for sure. You should just stay here and eat things from your garden."

*"I had rather be killed for a Picasso than a tomato,"* Gertrude said.

# PROVE IT'S RIGHT TO KILL

Oakland, October, 1990. The Gulf War loomed, there was talk of a draft. Gabriel and his friends were turning eighteen. Joaquin and Elliott's mothers, my son, and I staked out 14th and Broadway with signs quoting Gandhi and John Lennon.

*An eye for an eye makes the whole world blind.*
*You may say I'm a dreamer but I'm not the only one.*
And: *Honk if you love peace.*

The Bay Area and then national news media covered our vigil, which swelled to five hundred, six hundred, eight. Toddlers in strollers held signs that said "*Moms vs Bombs.*" Black families marched with huge American flags—high school yearbook photos of a boy or girl sewn into the stripes, their young faces in the stars. *The Oakland Tribune* printed a story about deployed U.S. soldiers flying to Saudi Arabia on the same planes as supplies of body bags. The army could have cut costs and just put those kids into bags right here at home. Our neighborhood newspaper interviewed eighteen-year-olds about the war. Gabriel was exploring conscientious objector status.

"Why should I have to prove it's wrong to kill?" he said. "They should have to prove it's right."

The U.S. Army Enlistment Center was doing a brisk business a block away—young men entering the building to enlist, angry protestors (including Gabriel) yelling at a line of armed soldiers holding bayonets two feet away.

"You're killing them! They're cannon fodder!"

A Public Enemy poster near the Broadway entrance to the recruiting station said in heavy block letters dripping with red: *I Got A Letter From The Government The Other Day.*

In my path to the demonstration, I saw the mangy blanket, then the paper cup, then the sign: *Hav a nise day*, the *y* of *day* falling off the cardboard's right edge—so it says, *Hav a nise da*. Plan ahead, I silently instructed the homeless. I imagined a cluster of ragged folks about to improve their lives as I teach them about spacing and spelling.

A woman, gray as the sidewalk, cradling a wrapped-up bundle against the cold. I dug out a few dollars and all my change meant for our Parents Against The War donation box.

"How's the baby doing?" I asked.

Carefully, the old woman peeled the ancient blanket back. Inside was the most beautiful baby I had ever seen. Blue eyes wide open, long lashes as if painted on, perfect skin, rosebud mouth, nose not running in this cold.

"That's a doll," I said.

The mother said, "Dolls gotta live too."

# EUCALYPTUS

Even though our house was surrounded by eucalyptus trees, bamboo, and flowering quince, I craved more seclusion, more quiet. I would move to Oregon, where it would be cheaper to live, giving me more time to write the poems gathering in me. Gabriel would join a group house in San Francisco.

He told his friends, "I turned eighteen and my mother ran away from home."

A young couple bought our house twenty days before the fire ravaged the Oakland/Berkeley hills, sudden torches of burning racing to the next crown of long papery leaves. They just had time to get out with their dog and the wedding album. I was in my new home, an old farmhouse in Grand Ronde, secluded in acres of grown-up Christmas trees. I hugged the radio praying, *Don't let the Claremont burn.* Eyewitnesses were saying if that sprawling majestic hotel burned, the fire would consume all of Berkeley.

Gabriel sneaked through security to see if anything was left of our house. Saw smoldering, foundation, chimney. He slept for a night in the bamboo stand, which did not burn. He'd lived there eight years, longer than anywhere else.

"And then," he told me on the phone, "in the ashes where the walnut tree and blackberries had been, I saw a little bouncing ball. Yellow-green," he said, "that yellow-green color you hate. You got it for me."

In his bouncing-ball phase, the walls leaped with red, blue, purple, every color—marbleized, neon, iridescent—stretching the limits of elasticity. The living room sizzled with blurred spheres of bouncing. Despite my dire predictions, he never broke a lamp. He filled his pockets with bouncing balls, went to the homeless streets, at Telegraph and Dwight Way, fished out a ball, and said "Would you like a bouncing ball?" The men stared blankly as the boy bounced the ball in front of them. They almost always took the ball, snatching it as though it was a trick.

Gabriel said, "Even though I left before the fire, I am homeless now because my house is gone. I thought my eyes were playing tricks on me, but there it was, in the ashes, yellow-green, perfectly intact."

# THE LAST BEAUTIFUL THING

Gabriel wanted to see if the homeless noticed more beauty than the homed. He took his camera to the streets of San Francisco and Berkeley and asked people, *What was the last beautiful thing you saw?*

STREET PERSON: "The last beautiful thing? Define beauty."

GABRIEL: "It's whatever you think it is."

STREET PERSON: "That doesn't sound right…Do you mean women?"

GABRIEL: "Anything you saw recently that was beautiful."

STREET PERSON: "How recently?"

GABRIEL: "Whatever you can remember."

STREET PERSON: "How do I know it was the last beautiful thing? What if I say that pretty girl over there and then I see something even more beautiful?"

Gabriel asks the question of a twinkly-eyed, white-bearded man in a slouchy hat. He looks like Walt Whitman.

STREET PERSON: "The last beautiful thing…Impossible to pinpoint it, my good man, there's beauty all around."

A young mother is balancing a baby in a polka-dot onesie on her hip. The answer to the question dawns on her before our eyes. "Him! He is the most beautiful thing."

Then a woman in a store full of trinkets, a baby over her shoulder.

"The last most beautiful thing?"

She looks around the store, trying to come up with something, behind her a display of beaded necklaces. Every time I see the film, I pray, don't say something you can buy. Look what's in your arms.

She says, "I'm stumped. You got me." The camera stays with her, waiting. "Oh, I know—the view from the Marina. Is that good?"

Some people took the opportunity of the camera's attention to tell their life story, as if auditioning for something.

STREET PERSON: "The last beautiful thing? Like to help you out, dude, but you caught me on a bad day. My girlfriend left me. We had to break up 'cause she was seeing someone else. I'm still hooked on her. I can't believe this happened. It's gonna take a long time to get over. Is there another question?"

Gabriel asks the question of an especially bedraggled young man.

STREET PERSON: "I've been on the streets since I was fourteen. I didn't know what debt was. I never heard of suicide."

The camera follows him as he walks away in the middle of the street.

A handsome young man with dreamy eyes and a foreign accent.

"The most beautiful thing? Does it have to be in America?"

GABRIEL: "Anywhere."

The street person doesn't speak. He smiles, his face radiant.

Gabriel keeps filming, then moves on: "Last beautiful thing?"

STREET PERSON: "The sunshine. Well, I think it's pretty amazing that the sun is one of billions of stars in this galaxy which is one we know now of fifty billion galaxies in the universe, up from ten, because of the Hubble Space Telescope and these are expanding, so the sunlight is a key term for the *siriah* in Sanskrit, sun, the source of all light and fire. And energy. And so it's a very powerful physical reality, the speed of light—186,000 miles a second and it's also a powerful symbol, so it works on many levels simultaneously and I think because of the integration of multiple levels of meaning and perception that I connect with sun and sunlight, beauty, in my opinion, has to do with aesthetic proportion and through a deep understanding of the sun, physically and metaphorically, you arrive at a beautiful universal proportion which I would identify with beauty, aesthetically. In fact, all the contradictions and problems of the universe are resolved in sunlight and in fire, as a matter of fact."

He leans back, beaming.

Gabriel moves on. "Last beautiful thing?"

"The sun. The sun on my back."

Gabriel told me, "Most people overall said the sun, or sunset. Most men said a woman; most women said their children. After those generalities came the unique stories, and as I expected, they were mostly from the homeless."

STREET PERSON: "A cloud. And you know what it was? It turned out to be Jesus Christ holding his hands out. [Pause] Can I interest you in a map of the city?"

OLD WOMAN: "I saw a Quarter Pounder through the window at McDonald's—that was beautiful."

We're in an art gallery. A sleek stylish woman.

GABRIEL: "What was the last beautiful thing you saw?"

Woman, smiling, "A painting."

GABRIEL: "Which painting?"

She moves to a portrait of an idealized young woman hugging an idealized cat. "It's for sale."

GABRIEL: "How much?"

WOMAN: "One hundred thirty-five thousand."

At the Powell Street cable car turnaround, two teenagers, shiny and round-faced as the moon. The boy speaks first:

BOY: "The last most beautiful thing." [Pause] "I'm thinking." [Pause] "I want to give you a really substantial answer." [Long pause] "Upper Yosemite Falls! I went to the end of the trail and climbed over the bar that keeps you from falling over the cliff and sat there with my legs dangling over and the waters of the falls rushing by one thousand feet straight down."

The girl speaks in present tense, as though she were still there. Her fingers move like playing a harp.

GIRL: "All this mist is coming to us, like little angels dancing around. And I looked at the valley and there were two rainbows. We want to welcome you to dinner."

"That's sweet," I said to Gabriel when we watched the film together. "Did you go?"

He said, "Mom, they're Moonies."

The question is *the last beautiful thing*, but some people repeat "the last *most* beautiful thing," raising the ante. Like beautiful isn't enough—it has to be the best. The eager and the diffident, the baffled and the smug—we are all starved in the end for what we think, what we saw. \*\*\*

STREET PERSON: "...the last beautiful thing? Is that all you want to know? Ask me something else. I haven't been paying attention to beauty lately. Why are you doing this? Will you be coming back tomorrow?"

A man with a shopping cart full of cans. Gabriel asks the question. The man asks for it again, looking into the camera intently. He has a pronounced speech impediment.

STREET PERSON: "I was at the Cliff House and these people were looking through the telescope and they walked away and I looked and they hadn't used up their quarter. I looked through the telescope at the water and there was a great ship right there, a Navy ship. That was thirteen days ago. It was a Tuesday."

Gabriel said to me, "See how he was looking at me? He was reading my lips. He was deaf. He gave the most detailed answer of anyone and exactly when it happened. All he has is his vision. With his cart full of cans, it was clear this man earns his livelihood off what others throw away. His memory of beauty was fueled the same way, by gleaning what others had thrown away—the quarter in the telescope, the beautiful view. He took their trash and made it a gift, which fed his soul."

Gabriel told me by the third day, he felt *The Last Beautiful Thing* was his calling—he had to ask the question. I imagined him going home on BART after a day of shooting, wanting to ask his fellow passengers the question. I imagined him shaving in his mirror, asking the question of himself.

At the end of the film, the credits and title are scratched into the sidewalk where most of the people sat. The lettering is primitive. The last thing we see is a quote from Dostoyevsky: *Beauty will save the world.*

## OREGON

Old farmhouse in Grand Ronde, ten acres of grown-up Christmas trees. Space, fragrance, quiet. The moment I sank into my vintage sofa, the poems spoke. I could barely write fast enough, they *weren't* lost or forgotten. They were inseparable from me.

A small press publisher in Berkeley, Creative Arts Book Company, presided over by Donald S. Ellis, knew me from my calligraphy. That's how *Miss Coffin and Mrs. Blood* was born. What good luck. I changed my usual wimpy voice for the readings. Driving on Highway 18, I belted out "Old Man River," trying to sound like Janis Joplin.

*Sandy Diamond*

# WOMEN WHO HAD DONE IT ALL

The Women's Correctional Center in Salem, Oregon. I sat at a scarred table in a locked room with a prison writing group, women who had done it all, including murder.

When I read about the mangled heart of a bracelet on the street, they shouted, "Damn right!" "You said it, sister!"

"Yeah, that's how I felt when my boyfriend slugged me and I brained him with the frying pan!" They had stories that made me look like Little Bo Peep.

After our hour was up, one inmate, instead of following the others out of the room, turned and came after me.

"I already *know* how to write!" the inmate called to me.

"That's enough, Stella," the guard said, pushing me to the exit.

"Leave!" she said to Stella, pointing, a walkie-talkie on her belt.

Two more guards, men this time, appeared behind Stella, locked her arms, steered her yelling through the cell door.

In the pat-down room, I saw a stack of RULES FOR VISITORS. I took one home, a souvenir of trying to do less harm than good in this world. I didn't know enough yet to be a writing teacher. I should have said, "Details! Details are everything. Don't just be angry—tell us what color the frying pan was—as black as the eye he gave you? Implicate everyone you can in your story. Tell it through the eyes of the dog, the cat, a stranger passing by your house in the night wondering, 'Was that a cry?'"

When I got home, I wrote this for Stella and me:
    already know how to write
    *Visitors shall wear*
    I'm good
    *conventional clothing*
    really good
    *not unduly suggestive*
    What I really want
    *or tight-fitting*
    is to be published
    *No halter tops or see-through, sheer fabrics, loose weave—*
    the world out there
    *Wearing underclothes*
    needs to hear
    *is required*
    what I have to say
    *Exposing an undue amount of flesh*
    It's written down I tell you
    *shall not be allowed*
    I could give it to you
    *No physical contact*
    You could give it to a publisher
    *except a brief embrace*
    You are out there!
    *and kiss upon meeting and leaving.*

# THINGS STANDING IN FOR OTHER THINGS

I visited a friend in a mental facility in Salem. We were in a writers' group together. Susan Spady was an original, her poems startlingly compassionate. She identified with everything hurt—a dead bird decomposing on her daily path. Along with her wrenching poetry, she was an imp beneath a veneer of tranquility. My qualification as a former mental patient bound us together. At the psychiatric hospital, I wore my sanest demeanor. I could hardly believe the nurse let me take Susan outside with me for half an hour. We kept straight faces until we were on the street. We'd pulled a fast one, the imposter leading the deranged.

It was windy. We turned our collars up—like secret agents, we told each other, giggling. I was smoking Virginia Slims then—long, narrow, elegant, flickering on and off with the match's trembling flare, which kept extinguishing in the wind. We didn't realize we were re-enacting the advertisements for Virginia Slims: women breaking decorum by sneaking a smoke. Maybe we could be in an ad and make some money that way. I had folded in my pocket the "For Visitors" handout from the nurses' station. Susan and I read aloud the items visitors were asked not to bring to the patients:

*Any weapon, knife, or tool of any kind*
*Safety pins, bobby pins, needles, or razor blades*
*Rope, clothesline, or twine*

"What about hatchets?" Susan started it. "Axes, crowbars, blunt instruments?"

"Disguises," I said, "Halloween costumes, masks of Nixon, beards, wigs, surgical masks, Groucho Marx glasses, mustache, and nose!"

"Oh damn!" she said, "That's the one I wanted!"

"Nothing from a magic tricks store—"

"Nothing that pops up out of a box without warning."

"A good rule of thumb is if it's maddening to you, it's maddening to them."

Susan was a master of the deadpan. She intoned, pretending to read from the handout, "Our patients are heavily medicated and any practical joke may throw them off-kilter. The theory that a mild scare will snap a mental case out of an affliction was disproved in the sixties."

You would think a sense of humor, brilliant poetry, a child would save someone from madness. But no. That isn't how it works. Voices told Susan to take her life, told her exactly how. So ghastly, I vowed not to tell anyone. And I haven't. And I won't here. I'll just say her method of getting out of this world had nothing to do with the instruments that so amused us that brief luminous day.

"No Ideas but in Things" (William Carlos Williams)

*Let's pretend this is the toothbrush*
*that the egg carton loves so much.*

*—Emily (age 2)*

    And so, it is in that other world—
    things love each other, even
    things that are standing in
    for other things, for every-
    thing stands for love, for some-
    thing beyond itself which shines
    through it. And so we must ask
    what it is we stand for, what shines
    in us, through us, and if no-
    thing, then why, and what
    have we forgotten; ask how
    we could forget the light in every
    cell and atom, forget this world,
    this dance of light and love—
    forget that by pre-
    tending, we make it so?

*—Susan Spady, The Body Open*

Sandy Diamond

# THREADS ONCE SEWN TO SOMEONE'S COAT

Sheridan, Oregon: A large poster of her face—those haunted eyes—mounted by the church door. The face that stands for six million faces. My job was to record attendance. I pushed a button each time someone entered. Not so easy as you'd think—people came and went and came back. This was very upsetting. No one to ask how to handle this. Or a group surged past *Historical Context* without looking, spreading out to the flashier displays where they disappeared into the already-counted.

A busload of children. The first thing they saw was the yellow star, threads once sewn to someone's coat, still hanging like little stick figures. I detained them and their teachers while I secured an unassailable count. The children examined the bits of everything. They loved every piece of information they could get about Anne Frank as though she'd been a chum who'd had a great adventure. They watched the movie. Anne Frank erased the answers to her crossword puzzle, gave it to her mother as a gift. They continued this practice back and forth, until Year Two, when the paper tore. Crossword puzzles: the meaning of words. The paper disappeared and the words disappeared and meaning disappeared. And, of course, life. But then the play and the movie came out so she lives that way.

When the children came to the camp section, the faces of the inmates were hard to make out, but they spotted the numbers right away. Noses pressed to the glass, they yelled,

"That's a three."

"No, it's an eight!"

They made up a little game: who could find the highest number.

# THE YAMHILL RIVER

I had a neighbor named Nick who had a dog named Frank, a Jack Russell terrier. They lived in a makeshift shack on the woodsy bank of the Yamhill River. Frank would dash through the high tasseled grass where Nick and I basked in next to nothing. And Nick threw sticks in the rushing stream for Frank to fetch, speed back so that Nick wrestled the stick from Frank's jaws, both of them panting. And Frank shook icy drops of the Yamhill River on our August skin, our warm August skin.

An Olympic swimmer in '72, Nick's streamlined torso still triangular, his manhood like a first-class medallion. And the river churned and the river hummed. We were both libido and he wasn't wearing his what-keeps-it-on? skinny black Speedo.

When it was Nick's turn to freestyle at Munich the following day, the Black September *fedayeen* massacred the Israeli team. The United States whisked Nick away along with Mark Spitz and his seven gold medals. Those years of training—no drink, no dance—he never got another chance—too old four years later. The touring company of *Fiddler on The Roof* had performed for the Israeli team the night before.

The Yamhill River's cold and swift, the air warm, caressing. Peaceful to laze on the peaceful shore and not think of anything at all, not think of anything.

I don't live in Yamhill County anymore. Nick, I hear, is in Hawaii. Frank's at his eternal rest, resting on his laurels. Well, all dogs die, but the Yamhill River lives on my skin, the best damn river for throwing a dog's stick in.

*Sandy Diamond*

# SLEEPING WITH EVERYONE IN SIGHT

It turns out mine was a classic case of manic depression. As soon as I work it into the conversation—because it's fashionable these days, you know—people nod, they know all about it. No one lifts an eyebrow; no one backs away. Everyone knows someone who—the buying sprees, the talking jags, the guns, sleeping with everyone in sight—all this is now practically the norm. It all happened fifty years ago…*fifty years! Let go of it!* But classic *means* enduring.

On the Lower East Side, there was this bum—we called them bums and winos then—who raced me for a long butt, still smoking on the sidewalk. He beat me to it, eyed me, then, bowing—handed it to me. Don't tell *me* chivalry is dead.

Now at parties where no one smokes—not even outside—I chat up therapists to see where their heads are at. One evening over halibut and chardonnay, a poet-doctor said his own brother was bipolar—that's what they call it nowadays. He waggled his fingers in the yo-yo space between us. "ECT is much more humane now," he said softly.

If I went back to New York, would I see her on a side street, paint on her black coat, battered portfolio under one arm, braids unwinding in the wind, smoking, pigeon-toed, trying not to step on the cracks? And seeing me, bent and slow, would she think, *Hey! That old lady's got my hair!*

The girl I was still walks past tenements, talking to herself. Remember the movies on Broadway, how after the last show when the ticket booth was empty, they dimmed the marquee, we swooped into the lobby, plucking long butts from the sculptured urns of sand. Remember the fire at the Modern when the big *Water Lilies* burned and we stood there in the night, the streets full of artists and wept.

## PRIMITIVE LIFE FORMS

Young and hungry in California, we
brought home chopped liver from Tastee
Take-out. Famished, we squeezed too hard & the
filling squirmed
from the bread to our laps, maddening us
with passion & we ran with the food
to the bed which then was a chunk of foam
covered in paisley.
The design of paisley suggests
primitive life forms wriggling toward each other &
it was California & we loved
chopped liver & it was the last time
our bodies would ever be so delectable.
Three decades later, paisley's back in style.
And a caraway seed stuck in the teeth
still recalls that long-past midnight snack. In fact,
the mere phrase midnight snack takes me back
to the paisleyed foam in that California flat—
Oh the cat clawed at the door
& the ants were thick as flies
& we didn't care who had more pickle
or that they left the napkins out
& the coleslaw smelled suspicious
& the frilly-headed toothpicks

*Sandy Diamond*

& the olives slick ball bearings—
though we knew that for real egg creams
it has to be New York,
we felt we got our money's worth
'cause they never hold the mayo
in the delicatessen of love.

# HOW TO BE A HUNCHBACK

The closest market to Grand Ronde was The Big Apple in Willamina. I'm always on the lookout for tall people in the supermarket, since the powers that be put my favorite foods on the top shelves. Actually, they only need to be taller than me. Men love to be asked to reach or lift something; women are used to helping. Once, a couple had a fight over who would reach the MaraNatha peanut butter for me. The man put a hand on a jar of chunky; the woman pointed to the smooth and creamy.

"This one?" he asked.
"She means this one," she said.
"She pointed to this one."
"I've got it."
"This one's a better buy."
"It isn't better if she doesn't like it."
"You always force your opinions on other people."
"Here you go, little lady. Enjoy."

---

"Can you lift that jar of Bubbies Kosher Dill Pickles for me?"
I wasn't even afraid the guy might be an anti-Semite. I came to feel that instead of bothering people, I was doing them a favor. It's fun to phrase my request to give men a chance to demonstrate their strength. Women instantly become my mother because it's obvious I don't know what I'm doing. People hunger to help a small person. We are all here in the Big Apple in small-town America.

Once, there was no reacher in sight, only an ancient man, bent and trembling. He didn't look strong enough to lift a grape. I watched him for a minute, wondering if I should try the next aisle. But who am I to give up on anyone?

"Excuse me, sir, would you please see if you could reach that jar of Nutella up there for me?"

Before my eyes, he straightened up and, stretching his arm like Plastic Man, handed me the chocolate. Our fingers touched.

"That was easy," he said, smiling. "Anything else, as long as I'm here?"

Once, the honeydews were out of reach. I asked a man to roll a few down to me. He thumped and sniffed a dozen melons, then lifted one into my cart. The wan chartreuse skin was traced with wasp tracks.

"If it's sweet to the wasp," he said, "it's sweet to us."

Once, when I turned into the breakfast cereal aisle, a little boy dressed like a cowboy drew his toy gun on me.

"Stay where you are—you're under arrest!"

I let go of my cart and raised my hands. "But what did I do?"

"Everything! You're a girl!"

---

The parrot on my favorite sauce watched me trying to reach him on the top shelf. Two teenagers, tall as longing, levitated into my aisle, their hands in each other's back pockets as though to hold themselves down to earth. Effortlessly, the lovebirds plucked the Pickapepper from its perch and floated it into my cart. The frayed ends of their cutoffs caressed their thighs, reminding them of each other at every step.

"Anything else? These olives are good."

They were whispering by the Jams and Relishes. I heard him ask, "A hunchback—is that supposed to be good luck or bad luck?"

"Good luck," she said, "but you have to touch the hump."

God knows I wish them luck.

## HUNCHBACK MOVIES

The thing I loved most about the film *The Station Agent* was when the eight-year-old girl first sees the dwarf, hunched over, fixing the railroad track. You could see her taking in his differentness and trying to figure out a way to ask him about it. And the dwarf, bracing himself for the inevitable question. I felt the whole theater audience holding its breath with me.

Finally, the girl asks, "What grade are you in?"

---

Remember when *ET* is disguised as a ghost on Halloween? The *Star Wars* trick-or-treater stares at him through her costume's alien eyeholes.

"Who are *you* supposed to be?" she says.

That is the question. This bonsai dwarf of my life, this stammer, this tremor, this fatigue, this forgetting. This complaining.

Think of us when you're in an elevator and someone calls out, "Move back, please." The person in front of me doesn't know I'm there. We're all packed in that rising, falling dumbwaiter cage either inflicting damage or waiting for an apology.

McMinnville, Oregon: on the curb, waiting for the light to change—eye to eye with an eight-year-old, holding his mother's hand and staring.

"Are you a child?" he whispered and giggled.

The sign said *Walk*, the mother yanked him into the street and said, "Don't laugh at funny people!"

When it came time for me to leave Oregon, I was sad to go. The local theater was doing *The Wizard of Oz*. I could have been a Munchkin.

*Sandy Diamond*

# THE JOKE

Have you heard the joke about the hunchbacked woman and the man with a wooden eye? They each went to a singles' dance. The man sees the woman, sitting alone in front of the wallpaper. He lurches toward her and says, "Would...you...like...to...dance?"

Thrilled, she cries, "Would I? Would I?!"

And he cries, "Hunchback! Hunchback!"

I loved that joke when my back was straight and my dance card full. Maybe the band was playing Glenn Miller, "In the Mood." If she hadn't said the wrong thing and he hadn't taken it the wrong way, they could have danced a fox-trot. Maybe after a paper cup of punch—spiked with vodka—they'd remember snazzy moves from high school, before their injuries, when they were young and whole. Remember how Glenn Miller arranged that song? That trick ending that seems to be stopping—and the guys would dip their dates into a backbend until the girls' lovestruck eyes were upside-down—and then the song starts over again. This trick ending happens three times. It says: It isn't over. There's more.

*Never put a period where God has put a comma.*

—*Gracie Allen*

*Ohio's faraway now. What would it be like to go back, back to No-Touch Hill? It's really high. How did I climb it all those years, touching and not touching? An old woman now, poking my walking stick into the past. Looking up, I can see the nearest fronds of ferns still there. Still there! How is it possible, when I have changed so much? They've been there all this time, beaded with the jeweled thunder of my waterfall.*

## CALL IT YOUR LIFE

During World War I, artists' pigments were used for painting bombers. Slowly, all the painters ran out of paint. It still breaks my heart to think of it. They wrote to each other, asking, "Perhaps you have some extra blue?" I've seen the correspondence of an Impressionist who told his friends, "Pissarro is out of Alizarin! For God's sake, can you help?"

Matisse sent Bonnard two tubes of oil: Violet and Emerald Green. In letter after letter, Bonnard asked what he owed for the paint that Matisse meant for a gift—he couldn't bear thinking of his friend's landscapes without his favorite colors.

I wish I had been there when Braque or Picasso saw a scrap of blue paper in the wastebasket, plucked it out, smoothed the creases. What I love about collage is how the touching and not touching of torn edges suggest desire. And its promise of redemption: you arrange fragments into a pattern, call it your life.

# WHEN NO ONE WAS LOOKING

January 1947 on his deathbed, Bonnard asked his nephew to add some green to the lower-left corner of his last canvas, *The Almond Tree*, in full bloom. If anyone could paint from the next life, it would be Bonnard. When he visited his work in a museum or private home—when no one was looking—he'd take from his pocket a few colors and a brush and change ochre to rose or a garden chair to a bush. This practice became known as *bonnarding*. Imagine—to have a verb named after you! He was saying, *It's never over.*

---

War meant chopped onion too small to dig out of hamburger. My brother and I sneaked clots of wartime meat under the dining room table to our collie Tippy. Mother wondered to Daddy why the dog had such bad breath. Remember before the War when you could have all the ketchup you wanted, to drown out stuff you didn't like—onions to make the meat go further in 1943? There were no onions before the War; life was sweeter then.

# SANDY'S AFTERWARD

DR. JEKYLL & MR. HYDE

In 2006, *Chemical Imbalance: A Comic Adaptation of The Strange Case of Dr. Jekyll and Mr. Hyde* debuted at the Exit Theatre in San Francisco. Author: Lauren Wilson, Producer and Director: Matthew Graham Smith. Gabriel was Dr. Jekyll and Mr. Hyde.

Hyde's former friend: *He became too fanciful for me. He began to go wrong, wrong in the mind.*

"Pray tell me, do," asks Lady Throckmortonshire, "why must a blessing be forever entwined with a curse?"

Dr. Jekyll: "Please listen to me. I can't control my evil half any longer. The antidote no longer works and I'm helpless to fend off these horrid transformations!"

The respectable, debonair doctor—pink Victorian settee, crumpets, and restraint spasms into Hyde's hunchbacked crouch and warped grin.

Back and forth in breakdance tremors, Jekyll can't choose who he is anymore.

Robert Louis Stevenson's Jekyll:

*Think of me laboring under a blackness of distress no fancy can exaggerate…committed to a profound duplicity of life, a heady recklessness…*

*dissolution of the bonds of obligation. The drug…shook the doors of the prisonhouse of my disposition, the animal within me licking the chops of memory.*

Just before he dies as Hyde, the actor switches back to Jekyll and looks at the carnage he caused, with an expression of horror and heartbreaking sorrow.

I asked Gabriel how it felt.

He said, "I remember convulsing and letting the evil in, the agony, the pleasure, the battle, the surrender."

*Gabriel Diamond moves with ease from pedantic and proper to untamed and demented. His performance in the second act, when he is constantly changing from good to evil, is hilarious. When he is walking on the wild side, he looks like John Barrymore in the silent version of the classic and he has a voice like Boris Karloff on steroids.*
—*Richard Connema, Talkin' Broadway, San Francisco*

I used to think: I've been through this thing—I can help other people who are in it now. But it didn't work that way. When the afflicted told me their story, I was frightened. Their stories were too much like my story. Or too different. They did worse things than I did. I was afraid of them. Or they weren't crazy enough by my standards. The medicine that worked for me didn't work for them. They didn't find doctors as kind and wise as mine. I couldn't save anyone except in one way: if I told my story, they would know they weren't alone.

*A few years ago, Gabriel and I were talking on the phone and I asked him if he remembered any of my craziness when he was a child. A long silence followed. I squeezed the receiver to keep it from telling me something I didn't want to hear. Much too late, I prayed for absolution.*

*Finally, he said, "Sorry, Mom—all I remember is the love."*

*The End*

# EPILOGUE
## *By Dianne Diamond*

> For there is no friend like a sister
> In calm or stormy weather,
> To cheer one on the tedious way,
> To fetch one if one goes astray,
> To lift one if one totters down,
> To strengthen whilst one stands.
>
> —*Christina Rossetti*

This Christina Rossetti quote, always a strong seller when Sandy's calligraphy was exhibited, describes the very close relationship we shared most of our lives. My earliest memories, being more than six years younger, include her constantly drawing whether to make stylish clothes for my paper dolls or the most beautiful Valentine's and Mother's Day cards for our mom (the only one's mom chose to keep in her memento box). Many of you knew Sandy as her older self when she dropped to a mere 4'6" hunchback (a term she embraced and made fun and sometimes poignant poems about in her second published collection of poetry). But I can still see her in our large backyard playing softball with my older brother—her strong, straight, twelve-year-old-self hitting a ball so solidly, then running the bases with her braids flying behind her as she made it to home plate.

There was only that time when the manic-depressive episodes began in her early twenties and I was about sixteen, that I lacked the knowledge and compassion to understand why her behavior was tearing at the fabric of our family. I was never allowed to visit her; my parents never discussed why she was in a hospital. Worry about her filled all their attention. It was not until I found myself in college and began experiencing bipolar events that I began to understand what my exceptional sister had been going through. We began to write and talk in-depth. She was like a scout who had been sent out to warn me of the possible ambush that would derail so many of my plans.

I used to think of us as the teeter-totter kids. Fortunately, when one of us was in a depressed mode, the other was up. Or if one of us was heading into mania, the other would do their best to rein it in, usually to no avail before lithium. My other image is that of two people on the same side in a tug of war. One hand over the other, we were there to pull each other along the way. I pulled her to California; she pulled me to Northern California. Many years later, she pulled me to the Northwest. We saw each other through fearful times and times of great personal happiness and triumphs.

It has been more than three years since my sister passed away. When her son asked me to write this epilogue, he added that I was now the keeper of Sandy's memories, having known her from childhood, through the craziest of times, and spending our last ten years together in the creative and beautiful community of Port Townsend, Washington.

Now you are the keepers of her memories. This was Sandy's last gift to us. She was an alchemist who took the glories of her life, the deep love she left, added the mental and physical challenges she faced and spun it all into gold.

*Sandy Diamond*

# GABRIEL'S AFTERWARD
*by Gabriel Diamond*

Most people speak of Sandy as the artist, the writer, the performer, the teacher, and the friend. This will be about Sandy, the Mom.

For as long as I can recall, my mom was the happiest person I knew. She was always excited by new friends, new art projects, new writings: plays, poems, and performances with her band. If you've read this memoir, you would know it wasn't always that way. My mom was one of the lucky ones for whom lithium worked.

Here are some words that I shared at her memorial:

I remember her picking me up in sixth grade, driving that ancient VW bug. I could hear it going *putt putt putt* long before I could see her. As we drove past other kids, I would duck down, embarrassed by her. Oh, the cruelty of children!

In high school, I had a teacher who asked us all who our role models were. When I said I couldn't think of anyone, he looked at me and said, "Your mother." He clearly saw something I didn't. And of course, he was right.

She made her hunchback her badge of honor, her self-identity. This deformity that I used to be embarrassed by when I was a kid, she was proud of.

When I got a new set of friends in high school, they'd bond with her by having long conversations. They'd tell me. "Your mom is so cool!" That's when I finally began to realize what was obvious to everyone else.

My best friend, Joaquin, told me, "She never really figured out how to get angry at you." She would only be disappointed, but never angry. That look of disappointment was the worst punishment I ever received.

Growing up, there was a quote on the wall by Marianne Moore that she'd calligraphed: *The only cure for loneliness is solitude*. She'd always told me she never wanted to be in a relationship. In art school, she'd made a pact with God: "If you make me a great artist, I won't ask for love." That bargain was part of the lore I grew up with, until I realized that by having me, she'd manifested that love she'd been willing to renounce.

When I turned eighteen, it was she who moved out of the house. Wherever she lived, from Berkeley to Oakland to Oregon to Washington, she always made new friends, surrounded by adoring, creative, funny, and kind people. Yet she chose to live alone. A benevolent hermit, she had a collection of handmade signs she'd hang outside the front door, asking not to be disturbed so she could work uninterrupted. We joked about putting one of them on her grave. "Writing, or thinking about it. Please do not disturb."

She had a love affair with smoking. You know she used to smoke four packs a day?

She told me about how when I was four or five, I threatened to run away if she didn't quit. And she believed me enough to stop.

When I would come up to visit her in Port Townsend once or twice a year, we'd share a cigarette on the back veranda. It was her once a month ritual for many years. She'd brag about that one cigarette a month and with whom from town she'd shared it.

She used to have a brown to beige Pantone paint color sample palette with one shade checked so she could show people the color she liked her coffee so they'd know how much milk to put in it.

She made me French toast every single day for about ten years. No matter how many slices she gave me, I would always leave about half a slice uneaten. She never made me finish.

After Lizzy was born, my mom gave me a journal that she'd started when she was pregnant with me. I opened it up to a random page and read these words: "How alert you are, sweet tempered, yet your outraged cry when I changed you or was too slow at nursing time, you are full of spirit, demanding your due." As a new father, I could feel those words were medicine for me, yet I couldn't take it in. It was too much love.

Eventually, I was ready to read it cover to cover. Here's from an entry she wrote on her birthday, two months before I was born:

*And I show off my belly to my woman friends—soon my child, you shall know them, their voices, laughter, and hands holding you. How welcome, well that you come, you are welling up in me, precious offspring, warming in this ripest summer. What a lovely birthday I've had… And I heard from this night that we shall live in Berkeley.*

Sometimes, I feel like I was born on a gold mine, and it'll take a lifetime for me to uncover all the riches—like my life has been a series of unveilings, as the beauty is slowly revealed. In her art and words and deeds, my mom stockpiled a full life of goodness for me, and so many others.

In her last few days while she still had words, she was still intent on rearranging the art in her room at the nursing home. Her sister, Dianne, had brought all her favorite paintings and chatchkes to make the sterile room feel like home. My mom asked me to hang a massive abstract painting by a classmate of hers from art school in the fifties on the ceiling above her bed so she could look at it as she lay there. I told her it might not be safe, that it could fall on her, that the nursing home might not allow me to put holes in the ceiling. She said in a teasing tone, "Gertrude Stein had a painting on *her* ceiling." How I wish I'd granted her that dying wish. I know she would have for me.

In the last couple days, she began to have visions, waving her arms in a panic as if trying to brush some unseen fabric from her face "What's this green and red veil? Gabriel, did you put this here?"

I don't have memories of her days of insanity that were described in this book. She discovered lithium when I was five, before my memories. But in the throes of those final days, I saw how the delirium and fears could rise up and take over. Watching her cry out in fear, not knowing how to help, was that what her parents felt? Were they also blaming themselves for not being able to make it better?

She made it through all that madness and self-destruction and became a great mother.

Now, as I parent my daughter, Lizzy (formerly known as Skyler) at some particularly difficult moment, I'll often ask myself, "What would my mom do? Which road would she have taken?"

During my mom's final days, after she had chosen to stop eating and drinking, I asked her what she wished she could do if she had more time. Without a pause, she said she wished she could finish her memoir and give Lizzy "one last hug."

I promised her I would get the memoir published, and here it is. It shouldn't have taken me 4.5 years, and might never have gotten done without the help of some dear friends and family. Candice and Dianne: thank you.

Although Lizzy was still down in California, I knew I could help her with at least one request. So, I opened up her memoir on my computer and I said, "We can work on it now."

And we did. Despite all her complaints about not being able to remember things, she was incredibly sharp. I would read to her and she'd pause me to make suggestions. At one point there was a combination of words, and then a couple pages later she said, "I think I said that already." I said, "No, no you didn't." Just to be sure, I went back to look, and she *had* said it earlier. She was catching things I wasn't. There was something about reading her own words aloud to her that made them come alive for me in a whole new way. There is no audience like a mother.

After we'd spent a few hours on it, all of a sudden, she'd say, "Get me some water." It was like she found the will to live again. That night at 3 a.m. while I was fast asleep on the floor, she called out to me:

"Gabriel. Gabriel!"

"What, Mom? What?"

"Let's keep working!"

"Alright. Let's do it…okay, where were we?"

"Page thirty-eight…"

It was what she wanted to do, to finish.

Toward the end, she started to ask me what was going to come after this. She'd never been interested in the afterlife before that.

"After I go, you could all have a party."

I asked what we'd do at the party.

She said, "Eat ice cream."

I asked which flavor and she said, "Chocolate."

---

I had asked a friend what advice she had for how I should show up in those final days. She said, "Let her hold you."

The sweetest thing my mother said to me in the last couple days, as I laid my head on her lap while she gently patted my head was, "You're a good boy."

Her last words were, "Get me out of here."

After we buried Sandy, as I was going through her scraps of paper with snippets of calligraphy, I found this quote: "Blessed is the heart with strength to stop its beating for honour's sake." With this memoir and the art that she left us, she continues to bring us all closer to *Bliss, Danger, and Gods*.

So, for me, I'll always remember her as Mom. Sandy Diamond was more than the artist—she was a mother who unconditionally loved me, and the art she left behind is proof.